Accomplished

2016 Poetry Collection

Published by
The America Library of Poetry
P.O. Box 978
Houlton, ME 04730
Website: www.libraryofpoetry.com
Email: generalinquiries@libraryofpoetry.com

Printed in the United States of America.

THE AMERICA
LIBRARY OF POETRY

ISBN: 978-0-9966841-1-8

Contents

Poetry by Division

Accomplished

In memory of two of our student authors,
Liam Jessin and Benjamin Lynne Carrasquillo III

I Am From
by Liam Jessin
(May 15, 1999 – March 30, 2012)
Poem written during 6th grade

I am from beds, pillows, showers and baths
I am from a broken swing set and a basketball hoop
I am from schools, parks and beauty all around
I am from "bon appetit" and "quiet, I'm sleeping"
I am from dumplings, rice, turkey, ham and cranberry juice
I am from my grandparents and my parents
I am from summers in France
I am from new lungs that breathe in my chest
I am from the Angel that gave them to me
I am from memories of my family that lived before me

Untitled
by Benjamin Lynne Carrasquillo III
(August 16, 1991 – September 21, 2013)
Poem written during 12th grade

I wake up every morning
And am excited to what the day brings
Will my aspirations be shut down
Or will they be given wind beneath its wings
Our thoughts, weighed down by the enemies in the media
Got us all thinking that everyone else has schizophrenia
When we begin to think, we unfold this façade
But when we do something they say we are forsaken by God
They teach us to read and write, but when we forget to cite
We get involved in a legal fight
Don't teach me so you can take what I make
Rather teach me so I can break
The confines of your mistakes and awake
The generation that's at stake
Call this a ploy
Or an eccentric young male defending the hoi polloi
But at the end of it all, I face myself asking if my squalls
Were worth placing my happiness on a shelf
But I know I'll have no regrets
Because I'll remember less than I forget

Foreword

There are two kinds of writers in the world.
There are those who write from experience,
and those who write from imagination.
The experienced, offer words that are a reflection of their lives.
The triumphs they have enjoyed, the heartaches they have endured;
all the things that have made them who they are,
they graciously share with us, as a way of sharing themselves,
and in doing so, give us, as readers, someone to whom we may relate,
as well as fresh new perspectives
on what may be our common circumstances in life.
From the imaginative,
come all the wonderful things we have yet to experience;
from sights unseen, to sounds unheard.
They encourage us to explore the limitless possibilities
of our dreams and fantasies,
and aid us in escaping, if only temporarily,
the confines of reality and the rules of society.
To each, we owe a debt of gratitude;
and rightfully so, as each provides a service of equal importance.
Yet, without the other, neither can be truly beneficial.
For instance, one may succeed in accumulating a lifetime of experience,
only to consider it all to have been predictable and unfulfilling,
if denied the chance to chase a dream or two along the way.
Just as those whose imaginations run away with them never to return,
may find that without solid footing in the real world,
life in fantasyland is empty.
As you now embark, dear reader,
upon your journey through these words to remember,
you are about to be treated to both heartfelt tales of experience,
and captivating adventures of imagination.
It is our pleasure to present them for your enjoyment.
To our many authors,
who so proudly represent the two kinds of writers in the world,
we dedicate this book, and offer our sincere thanks;
for now, possibly more than ever,
the world needs you both.

Paul Wilson Charles
Editor

Editor's Choice Award

The Editor's Choice Award is presented
to an author who demonstrates not only
the solid fundamentals of creative writing,
but also the ability to elicit an emotional response
or provide a thought provoking body of work
in a manner which is both clear and concise.

You will find "Strawberry Birthmark"
by Devany Shikiar on page 217 of Accomplished

2016
Spirit of Education
For Outstanding Participation

Ernest Becker
Middle School

Las Vegas,
Nevada

Presented to participating students and faculty
in recognition of your commitment
to literary excellence.

Division I

Grades
3-5

Sports
by Andres Hernandez

Balls, shoes, technique, skill, heart
That's really all you need
You don't have to read
But, you have to be quick on your feet
To just score or anything you need a ball
And I guess you could get it at the mall?
Team or not, hopefully you have fun!

Porky Pineapple
by Kylen T.

He lives in the forest.
He's not smart what's a thesaurus?
He does not like chorus.
He loves to eat fruit.
He has a best buddy newt.
His best friend's name is Loot.
And Loot is very cute.
He looks like a chipmunk.
For a test he would flunk.
Because his brain just sunk.
He loves to play!
He could do it all day.
He loves to play by the bay.

Fall
by Jayden Dachis

Fall weather is crisp and cool
Candy apples make you drool
Soccer season is in full swing
Each goal in the net makes me sing
Halloween is so much fun
Scary costumes make you run
Halloween means candy galore
You can't resist getting some more
Leaves fall off the trees
They get carried away in the breeze
Thanksgiving is a great time of year
Pass the gravy or I'll bite off your ear
Fall is one of my favorite seasons
And these are all of the reasons

Appledog
by Gianna Spadaccini

There is an Appledog in town
He is red and brown
He loves to jog
Like a frog.
He eats a shake
With steak that is baked.
He has spots by his eyes
He also looks at the sky.
He likes to play with kids
Who like to play with lids.

Farroxt
by Alisha Bourhill-Tumser

The Farroxt lives in a forest.
Its environment has trees, also with bunches of leaves.
With its fox head it hunts well, it is often called a bell.
It also has good running legs, while it plays a game called pegs.
But it often lets itself down because its big carrot body weighs it down
It wanders around looking for shelter while it looks for something to felter.
It also tries looking, for someone to be cooking.
It looks for prey and carrots but beware because it does not like parrots
Always looking for something to pull its chariot
So it can be called the Farroxt.

The Baller
by Ethan Deronet

I'm an awesome baller
Be dunking like Kobe
Think you can cross me up
Come here and show me
I jump shot left and right
The ball goes down the hoop
with the push of my might
You need to come and see with your own eyes
Just crossed up Carmelo
I know this guy ain't a fellow
I could layup all day and night
Make awesome 3's and swooshes they will be
Then shrug through the day and night, saying they were all right.

Summer
by Daniel Joseph

Summer oh summer it is anything but a bummer.
From the blossoming flowers of day to fireworks of night.
Hanging out with family, friends will be a blast
I wish I could stay in the past.
From relaxing on the beach to playing tag on the playground
summer oh summer I guess this is the end
all the memorable moments stuck in my head
my favorite season has come to an end.

Mike Gets Grounded
by John Quinn

Mike destroys buildings.
He is VERY naughty!
And he is only 12 years old!
He is very cold.
He never does what he is told.
And his mom and dad always say this:
YOU'RE GROUNDED!
He makes the chorus sound like mold.
And he always gets coal,
FOR CHRISTMAS!
(Sometimes he goes to jail)

Country Music
by Michelle Torres

This is an important art.
This is where all music artists start.
Therefore, there is a special role to play
Whenever they walk on stage.
Some make it big
Yet, others go unnoticed.
There is a huge amount of us
But some of us, are in the dust!
All of us are patriotic, hardworking, and blue collar
And we will ALWAYS afford a dollar.
We have bonded together
Never EVER apart.
Yes, this is country music
straight from the heart.

Unishark
by Pawel Nowosielski

The Unishark eats rainbows
After he plays his banjo
People say he's white
But he's really bright
He is very blue and he is polite
He is a foot runner and can take flight
As he hunts he has good sight

Sunshine and Silence
by Ava Greco

Where did the clouds go?
Did they float away?
Do they want to be somewhere else?
No clouds, no clouds, no clouds
Sky is clear like a blank page
Sounds of birds chirping a happy song
The sound of nothing
It's peaceful
Staring at a light blue sky
Makes me happy
Sunshine and silence.

Cupcakes
by Milan Elvie

Big cupcakes
Yummy cupcakes
Splendid, cute, pleasant cupcakes
Luscious, petite, witty cupcakes
Those are just a few!
Elegant cupcakes
Radiant cupcakes
Marvelous, glimmering, bright cupcakes
Moist, tasty, terrific cupcakes
Amiable cupcakes too!
Pink cupcakes
Purple cupcakes
And don't forget blue cupcakes too!
Last of all
Best of all
I love birthday cupcakes!

American Flag
by Jack Campbell

American flag blowing beautiful day and night
Fifty stars oh so bright
Showing Americans' pride tonight

When I Dance
by Jasmine Persaud

When I dance,
I lose myself,
I leave the room,
When I'm still there
When I dance,
It's like dreaming with my feet,
And as my mom says,
I dream on
When I dance,
I feel free,
I feel alive,
I can be me.
When I dance,
I can fly,
I can soar,
Up in the sky.

Baseball!
by Roberto Rodriguez

Baseball baseball!
Hit the ball.
Run to first or run through them all.
Baseball baseball!
Pitch the ball hard.
My position is a pitcher
Behind a baseball card.
Baseball baseball!
Hear the crowd shout.
Catch the fly ball.
And the umpires yell "OUT!"
Baseball baseball!
The season has end.
I'll practice all winter.
Until we meet again.

Sports
by Brenden Donnelly

Sports are great
even when you get beat
you always have fun
but you should've won
right when it begun

New Day With Spring
by Faraz Bhatti

A new day with spring
It's like a desert in the morning
The day goes quick without me noticing
I smell the beautiful roses and fresh air
I hear the birds chirping as the sun goes down
We wave goodbye
As the huge sun goes down something comes out
That something is called the moon
As the moon comes out we go in
I go to my room and lay on my bed
And look at the moon then
I close my eyes and say goodnight
While I wait for the next summer day

Mice Spill Checkers: The Not-So Reliable Spell Checker
by Zachary Gallardo

Eye gut an knew spill checkers
End as eye goes a long
Mice spill checkers well tells me
Watts write from watt E's wrung
It's jabs rev icing mime miss steaks
Each whirred well bee core wrecked
End owl my whir kiss air or free
'Cause every whirred E's checked
These poem well half know miss steaks
Four mine warts is owl write
Mice spill checkers sea that their E's
Know air ors inn it's site
Aisle gave D's poem two yew now
Know air oars that its gut
Mine checkers says its all core wrecked
Miss steaks oar hear? There knot!

Nom, Nom
by Naomi Kim

Great smell
Delicious, good, soft bread
It's amazing, came from a pig
Hot dog

Dezelle
by Fiona Slatina

The forest is where it resides
It can escape landslides.
It runs on the mountain,
it drinks from the fountain.
It plays in the rain
It has a big brain.
It is fast,
also very vast,
it is lean
and very clean.

Crystal Pink
by Adrianna Graziano

Do cherry blossoms turn to cherries?
Crystal pink flowers
Lots of trees as tall as poles
Cherry
Cherry
Cherry
Voices of people talking
Leaves blowing
A slight breeze
Peaceful sounds
Cars moving
Blossoms as pretty as diamonds
A sky as blue
as the Caribbean Sea
A silent breeze passes by
Bright sun, few clouds
Shadows of people
A clear day
no rain.
Do cherry blossoms hold nectar?

A Great Day
by Jack Polizotto

Why is it yellow in the middle?
Blue flowers with a yellow middle
Some clouds in the sky
Green grass
Lots of dirt
Hot-hot-hot
Birds chirping
People talking
A bright sun like a flashlight shining in your face
Breezy, breezy, breezy
When do they start to bloom?
Dogs barking
Some laughter
People having fun
Playing with friends–
A great day.

A Wave of Love
by David Larsen

Tap - tap - tap
I imagine his paws
walking over to me
I see
dog toys
dog food
A dog cage
Tap - tap - tap
The sound gets louder
and I feel
A wave of love with
that small white face
Then ... a fluffy dog
jumps on me
It's "Frankie"
as white as
a snowball
As sweet as
ice cream
That's "Frankie."

Peace
by Molly Jacobs

We need to share and play
We should not hurt others, we shall only be nice
The world needs no more bullying
I hope we will not have any more war

Reduce, Reuse, Recycle
by Mustafa Oudeh

Words we all know.
We may be only kids
But we will try, you'll see.
We recycle what we use.
Separate things and you should too.
Paper and plastic, glass and tin!
Go into your recycle bin!
We must start now. We cannot wait!
Quick or it will be too late!
We can save this planet.
It starts with you and me.

A Giant Tree
by Ana Lopes

A giant tree
So big and brown
As fall comes, the leaves fall out
A giant tree
So calm and silent
Can't hear a thing, that's how it's quiet
A giant tree
So many colors
They are red they are green that is what you see
A giant tree
So bold so true
You can tell them anything they won't tell you
A giant tree
So young so old
No matter the age you can trust them
A tree
There are so many
But only one is the best

Stars
by Amed Fallas

Stars are in the sky,
They twinkle every night.
Some stars explode,
Others are just there for show.
Now you see,
That stars are pretty and also very deadly

Weedake
by Kevin Bruenjes

Last night I had a stomachache,
When my sister saw a Weedake.
The Weedake scowled,
When my sister howled.
At the crack of dawn I awoke,
When I found my sister in a room full of smoke.
She said the Weedake hissed with power,
I said go poke a flower.
I watched it eat her,
The cat went outside and said purr.
The Weedake coughed her up,
He died, Mom asked did a snake come, I said yup.

Beauty Under Me
by Jordan Titus

How old are you, Tree?
Are you 10 ... 20 ... 30 years old?
Your grass around you sparkling like glitter
Your bark rough like a rock
Sun shining on your green leaves
How old are you, Tree?
Are you 40 ... 50 ... 60 years old?
Birds on your beautiful branches
Your thick, skinny branches
Swaying in the warm breeze
Sky above with no clouds
Your branches snap when I climb them
Birds singing their beautiful songs
Are you 70 ... 80 ... 90 years old?
How old are you, Tree?

Life Is a Maze
by Michael Shipman

Life is a maze you must go through
There is a shortcut you may not know
Be brave be yourself no one will care
Even though there's a shortcut it may be hard
Some people will try to make you fail
Don't listen to them their hearts are stale
There are also some dead-ends along the way
Sometimes decisions will lead you nowhere
They'll take the passage and tear it all down

The Pish
by Marisa Ibraimi

If you like pigs and fish
then you would like the Pish.
The Pish live in the water
but, they hate the otter.
They live in the cove
and they drove.
When they play
they stay by the bay.
"Dad can you stay home today,"
is what they say.

Middle School Worries
by Amarachi Ebere

Nervous, scared, and worried
On the dark, gray, stairs of middle school
Every step you take is a war you have to fight,
While the cold wind bites with frights.
To you it might not be as bad but, to me the horror just starts
With every new face and grin the horror just restarts
But when I saw the light of my friends' happy faces,
My worried heart began to beat with pace.
With field trips, clubs and activities the worry started fading again
Then I realized all of my worry was a piece of baloney,
I had met some friends new and old.
So what I learned that day was
It is not always bad you just have to have hope!

Peace
by Brennan McVey

Purposeful we want peace to be
Earth is where peace stars
Anti-war so no damage is done
Can do it! We have to believe we can do it
Environment should not be destroyed

Summer Is Beautiful
by Joey Mintel

Summer is fun
When you're out in the sun
It is really warm outside
during the carnival I go on the Riptide
It's so fresh in a pool
When you're out of school
The beach is so nice
When you are licking your Italian ice

Strolling Down the Street
by Tyler Chin

Feeling the sun
shining
like a bright light
in my eyes
I can hear
my friend napping peacefully
in his stroller
I peer out from my stroller
As my mom pushes me down the street
I see the sun setting
Orange
Yellow
Red
Then yellow again
Sun sun sun
I hear my mom's voice
and her
footsteps
tapping
on the ground.

I Am
by Andrew Young

I am a student in Mrs. Anderson's fourth grade class
I wonder why clouds are white
I hear laughter and cars on the streets of New York City
I see the Big Ben in England
I want to go to New York to see my cousins and family
I am a student in Mrs. Anderson's fourth grade class
I pretend that I'm at the Empire State Building
I feel intelligent when I get a 100% on a test
I touch the Eiffel Tower on a warm spring day
I worry that I'm going to be stranded in the ocean all by myself
I cry when an animal dies in a sad movie
I am a student in Mrs. Anderson's fourth grade class
I understand that when you graduate college, you get a job
I say do your best on a test, try your hardest, and that is all you can control
I dream to travel the world and see exotic people and places
I try to make no errors in baseball
I hope that my parents will let me get a hover board
I am a student in Mrs. Anderson's fourth grade class

Stawburry
by Elmedina Destani

The Stawburry is a muffled animal.
It hides in the tall green grass.
People say the Stawburry is a mammal.
But besides the point the Stawburry isn't mass.
It's small and red and green too.
Also, black don't forget that too.
It has leaves that are green moo.
Shuw, shuw, shuw Mooshroom it's not your story that's who
It lives in a forest, it hides from the predators.
It stays with its family.
And more that the Stawburry stays with its mom.
The Stawburry missed a bug with a peonly.
The Stawburrys are not easy to spot.
They're like the flash that is miniature.
They're as small as an ant but not as small as a dot
The Stawburry leaves the next when they're more mature.
They eat grass and most of fruits.
They also look like a ladybug so don't leave it.
A Stawburry is a flower but don't loot the size.
That's all for now so don't take me.

People and Places
by Gabrielle Mori

In private school there was a boy
He joined our group and brought his toy
In kindergarten I knew this girl
She had brown hair that wouldn't curl
In first grade I had this teacher
She had never made me sit on a bleacher
In second grade I met this boy
He made me laugh a lot with joy
In third grade I met an old friend
Today, our friendship still has yet to end
In fourth grade I had a new bunch
Whom I sat with and ate lunch
In fifth grade there's a whole new crew,
Mixed with the old, and mixed with the new
The higher grades, now I don't care
For that can get out of my hair
For these people and places I will cherish
For you never know when they will perish

A Welcoming Warmth
by Alexandra Bruno

How is she so beautiful?
Her green sparkling eyes
A perfect round nose
That brown, wavy hair
Straight white teeth and
tan skin
She always has a
welcoming warmth to her
The most beautiful
heart-warming laugh
you could ever imagine
As beautiful as
buds blossoming
into big, bright flowers
Beautiful
Beautiful
Beautiful
She makes my inner light
Shine bright
This poem is about one person ... My mom.

Peace
by Julia Johnson

Peace is kindness
Everyone wants peace, we just don't know it!
And if we keep fighting, we won't get anywhere in life
Create a world of happiness
Each one of you should help the world

My Very Best Friend
by Madison Langhorne

My best friends name is Veronica
and she doesn't celebrate Hanukkah
We are very best friends
Until the very end
When we are together
It's fun in the sun
Or really boring homework
Either way we're best friends forever
Together forever, it's Veronica and Madison

Bright Lights
by Darline Sanon

These bright lights I see
They're not me
I'm just a shy little thing
With nothing to bring
I depend on books
Stars depend on looks
I don't belong in Hollywood
I can't act like a star should
I don't belong on a red carpet
I don't even have my life set
These bright lights
Show pretty sights
Don't depend on me
There's nothing to see
I can't be a celebrity
I'm as quiet as a kitty
The bright lights
Make people feel right
I know what I want to do
If you have a problem with that it's on you

Remember
by Grace Chu

I remember when
I took my first step
And when I said hi.
I remember when I got my first baby tooth
And I remember when I got my first bike
Or when I went on my first hike.
I remember when I cried my first time
And I remember when I had the most happiness

School
by Demarco Haye

This is my first day at school, but
Will they take me to the bathroom?
But what if I get lost?
What if the kids are smarter than I?
What if we had a test and I'm the one who doesn't pass?
What if my teacher doesn't like me or trust me?
What if my teeth get loose and they all fall out?
What if I lost my lunch or someone took it?
What if they'll let me starve?
What if they say something and I don't understand?
What if they like me and didn't know?!

The Beat of My Heart
by Zahra Kiyara Burgess

Bum, Bum, Bum!
The beat of my heart is as loud as a drum.
All day long it goes
Bum, Bum, Bum!
I can't live without it and so it is true,
the blood in my body goes all the way through.
My heart beeps repeatedly,
and if it stops I shut down like a robot.
When I sneeze my heart freezes,
and when I get the hiccups I jump like a jack-in-a-box.
This system in my body keeps going because my heart keeps pumping.
All the tubes pump in and out blood so my body keeps moving.
Every body has a heart but mine is special you see,
my heart has its own type of rhythm.

I See a Turtle
by Sophia Farid

I see a turtle
It is so cute
It just came out of the water
And he's wearing a suit!

What Trees Do
by Ojuolape Odusanya

Oh, I wonder, oh, I wonder what trees do.
I see them every day, everywhere, even in my backyard too.
Do they grow apples, do they grow paper,
can they grow so high, that they touch the sky?
They are a pencil making machine, but that is not all they are good for,
they help the environment too. They also give us air (oxygen).
Oh if there were no trees, would I grieve?
But wait, they do grow apples and make paper.
Boy, we need these trees because, trust me, they are our lifesavers.
Now I know what trees do.

My Beloved Papa
by Benjamin Danlasky

I look up to the sky and what do I see ...
Why it's my papa looking over me
When I play ball I always stand tall
because I hear my papa say, "Benji, give everything your all."
Sometimes I stumble and sometimes I fall ...
but I never forget to keep my eye on the ball
You said do your best always, but you will get knocked down.
Just remember to get right back up ... minus the frown
I take pride in my work and know in my heart
that even though you're in Heaven we are never far apart
My thoughts and my prayers always include you
And I know my mom misses you a lot too
She tells me to always do the right thing because the right thing is true
I believe she learned that from you
I hope that if you can see me through a cloud,
you see me standing tall and that I make you proud
One day we will meet again but in the meantime I'll just pretend
I keep your picture next to my bed and pray for you at night as I bow my head
For it was my pleasure to have known you Grandpa, this much is true
I hope you know how much I love you

Comics
by Judah Farrell

When writing comics I often think,
Add some color so readers don't have to blink
Blood and gore for me are just too wild,
So instead I try to be a little mild
Of course there's punching, kicking, bombs, and blasts,
But at least on the next page I draw them with casts!
Last but not least I name the setting and state
And no need to tell me, I know it's great

Wrestle
by Tyrese Rivera

I wrestle
I wrestle WWE style
I wrestle WWE style with my brother
I wrestle WWE style with my brother outside
I wrestle WWE style with my brother outside at noon
I wrestle WWE style with my brother outside at noon every day
I wrestle WWE style with my brother outside at noon every day because it's cool
I wrestle

Summer, Summer
by Asahy Puerto

Summer summer, is almost here
Time for fun, and swimming gear.
Trips to the beach, trips are always so much fun,
Rub on lotion, perfect for my summer skin.
On my bike, or the pool,
And a sip of water keeps me cool.
My shades are on, and my flip-flops too,
In summer there is so much to do.
School is almost done, I am enjoying ice cream,
I love the summer.
Summer summer, time for fun,
We run all day, in the hot, hot sun.
Summer summer, jump in the pool,
And eat lots of ice cream to keep cool.
Summer summer, is almost here,
I can't hardly wait,
Let's give a big cheer to summer!

Dolphins
by Cecilia Boada

Dolphins
Two show off and get an applause.
Four swim low, under the flow
Six dive high, into the sky.
Happy.

Hades
by Thomas D'Arco

Hades was dark and filled with gloom
He tricked Persephone and became her groom
He ruled the kingdom of the dead
People feared him and all he said
The souls of the dead were not so merry
They came to the underworld in a ferry
A three headed dog guarded his home
From his world, souls could never roam

Candy
by Chelsea Young

My name is Candy.
Today I feel real dandy.
My mother is a lollipop.
My father is a Gummy Bear.
My brother is chocolate, you can smell him from anywhere.
My cousin Bubble Gum.
Has a sister who's a Dum-Dum.
But who am I?
Where do I belong in this big candy world?
Am I a Caramel Swirl?
I like to laugh.
Am I Laffy Taffy.
Or am I a Hershey's bar,
That is simple and classy?
Am I a big piece of black liquorice?
Or a red chewy Swedish Fish?
Do you see me as an M&M or Skittle,
That's so tiny and little.
I'm still finding out who I am. In this path called Life.
It's a sweet journey. And you know what, being Candy is perfectly alright.

Peace
by Frank Kasper

Powerful as fire
Excellent as diamonds and gold
As amazingly good thing
Caring as a mother
Encouraging like a teacher

Trees Everywhere
by Richard Blaise

Trees everywhere
Trees big and small
Trees here and there
Trees short and tall.
I love them all!
Acacia, crab apples and oaks
Trees are great folks!
Trees aren't just pretty
They brighten up the dark city
Trees also help us breathe
So go ahead and plant a seed!

Being Free
by Taylor Wallace

I bounce up and down
I go super high
I can tumble, I can flip
I think I can fly
I run in huge circles
Because I am free
No one will have
Control over me
In gymnastics you can
Do many things
Boys can tumble around
And twist on the rings
Girls (like me) flip on the balance beam
Because being in the Olympics is our ultimate dream
With my strength and commitment
I approach my sport with no fear
Because I am FREE!!

May
by Daniela Ruby

Beautiful breezes in the air
Slowly hitting my face
Sun is creeping out from behind the clouds
While birds are chirping their songs
Sun reaching for the early May flowers
Beautiful colors all around
Puffy clouds entering the scene
Rain offering a drink to the blooms
Tap-tapping the leaves on its way down

Connection To Nature
by Benjamin Malone

Be silent
Step slowly
And you may feel
The connection to nature
Everyone has a connection
But not everyone is aware of it
I hope you are
We are part of nature
She brings every living thing together
If you need help finding the connection
Just ask me

The Lonely Fountain
by Francis Foderaro

I'm at church I hear the bell bang in my soul.
I see my father dressed in all black
and me in a tie and jacket stare at him.
The bell rings and this time deeper in my soul.
I look down in the church fountain to
see gleaming yet sad and frowned coins.
I throw one in and as it hits the lonely bottom
The bell bangs once more.
And I see a tear drip down my father's face.
As I gulp and feel the bell
this time much deeper in my soul.
Because this time I know it is time
This time is a horrible time.

Summer Trees
by Samah Keshiro

The perfect green leaves
Sway from left to right in wind
As its flowers sing.

Nobody But Me
by Valentina Gonzalez-Pichardo

I am me
Nobody but me,
I can step on a base
Or I could go to outer space.
I can fly across the sky
I don't know why,
I can dance with all my might
Even on a starry night
All I know is I am me,
Nobody but awesome me.

Spring Has Sprung
by Angelina Mauro

Winter fading,
Birds once again humming to the swaying breeze.
Stark trees,
Become snug and tightly wrapped,
Newborn nature seeps through their casing
As they begin their journey.
The lustrous bright figure off in the azure tinted sky
Blanketing the fluffed figures high above.
Near the sedentary clear liquid,
The zephyr slowly swayed the sedated pond into a pebbled current.
Over time, the aged leaves have decayed,
Abundantly canvassing and enclosing the ground,
Caressing every single blade of grass.
But still, as many as there are, they slovenly coat the earth,
To be swept away by fresh gusts of wind from the flower filled season.
Coasting, the warmth rapidly descends
To heat all living creatures out of hibernation,
From the brusque ice and snow that was.
Even yet, the time has come, exuberant and all,
To encase joy and laughs, for a spring call!

Peace
by Brooke Zuravnsky

Peace means to be a bucket-filler
Everybody needs to stop fighting and cursing
Anyone who sees someone getting bullied should stop and help them
Choose the right thing
Earn peace instead of harm

Nature
by Anuoluwa Oluwakuyide

The cool rain washed over my face in the meadow
It encamped around me like a blanket
As rain rolled down my cheek, the wind picked up
like it was having a race against itself
The rain and breeze collided– nature seeming to have an inner conflict
The rain and breeze united, making a breathtaking scene of nature
In a flash, I was left in the middle of the meadow
staring up as if it would happen again
Nature is a beautiful thing

Wonder
by Caroline Eckardt

When the birds sing in the morning light,
I wonder if they are singing for the cause of joy or sadness.
As they fly freely through the air, with the wind carrying them to their destination,
I wonder if the humans can see them from the elevation they have reached.
I wonder if the leaves want to be on the trees filled with chlorophyll,
Or on the ground showing their true colors, as they slowly crumble away.
Maybe the water wants to be something else?
Something more useful, or that has more meaning.
But the water doesn't realize what it does!
Almost like how I feel.
Pointless, in the world.
Yet, I don't know what I'm capable of.
So here I sit, thinking that all things are living.
That every detailed thought should be known by all ... Living and dead.
For the moss that grows on the smallest of rocks,
Should be treated as if it is as important as anything else.
Or the small acorn on the shed that is ready to fall to pieces,
Wants to be heard, just as the moss.
Someday people will understand how I feel.
How other things feel. I wonder.

Plants
by Alexandre Rodrigues

Trees
Tall, Leafy
Moving, Standing, Dancing
Brown, Branches ... Small, Wide
Sitting, Growing, Waving
Green, Peaceful
Bushes

Jump
by Joseph Sneyers

walking slowly
across the elevated surface
jump
twisting, turning
tumbling through the air
hold your breath
splash
flying through the water
down, down to the bottom
thump
need air
swim up
gasp

Compassion
by Elaina Sta Maria

People can show compassion.
Anyone can do it!
Be kind to one another just believe it!
Don't laugh at someone, help them instead.
Laugh with one another but not while calling them egghead!
Don't say mean words to other friends or strangers,
who knows, people might not help you when you're in great danger!
So look deep down in your heart, not on the weak side of your heart,
but the strong one.
A friend waiting for you is shown,
she or he might be alone.
But I know that, that person will have compassion for you.
So have compassion for them too!

Peace
by Leo Lanzone

We need fewer bullies
And more respect for each other
We need to include everyone
And no more war!
Stop fighting at school
And hold each other up
We need to treat the world better

A Summer's Day
by Alexis Jorge

Going to the pool is so fun.
I jump in the water
Under in the sun.
Then, it's time to eat.
My mouth waters for a sandwich and chips
And an ice cold lemonade in all this heat.
Later, I go to the park.
My friends come and say, "Hi."
We play until it gets dark.
A summer's day is extremely fun
Laughing and playing all day in the sun.

Obstacles
by Aleena Kuriakose

When there's a challenge, face your fear,
Turn your mistakes to a steer.
Believe and keep true to your heart,
Wash away your past to a new start.
Try your best,
Never get depressed.
Keep moving on,
Your accomplishments will be done.
If you know you can do it,
Your path will be lit.
In the blink of an eye,
You can reach high.
Believing is the gateway to your goals,
You will discover your true roles.
Keep on going no matter what you face,
Move forward, life is like a race.

Soaring Sheep
by Faith Carhuff

The sheep jump over my bed,
they soar above my head.
One, two, three, four, five,
counting up, up, up.
Six, seven, eight, nine, ten,
counting up, up, up.
I think it is sleep time.
Goodnight ...

Birds
by Hezekiah Ibarasa

What are birds without,
Their feathers for is that not what makes them fly
They fly so high that they are invisible to the naked eye
They shower like any mammal would but yet they are
Considered different because of the feathers they groom,
Are they not in our ecosystem, if not I must
Be feeling blue.
For what if we were like them, like angels in the sky
Would we be discriminated that is a question I continue to ask myself
Why?

Dominican Republic
by Jayson Morton

First, we got on a bus.
What a fuss!
When we arrived we saw our plane,
It was in the takeoff lane.
It took three and a half hours to get there.
The pilot said, "We're hitting rough air."
I got to have fun,
While relaxing in the sun.
I went in the blue water,
In a game, I won a quarter.
The music was played by the band,
They were set up on the sand.
Our trip was awesome,
We were a happy foursome!

Paint
by Victor Santana

I paint
I paint animals and pictures
I paint animals and pictures by myself
I paint animals and pictures by myself on Saturdays
I paint animals and pictures by myself on Saturdays at home
I paint animals and pictures by myself on Saturdays at home because it's fun
I paint

My Country
by Julia Schlesinger

Standing as an American, proud and free
Looking at the flag right in front of me
I say the pledge confidently
Living in a great country
Being American is amazing to me
Soldiers marching, fighting for me to be free
Standing on Capitol Hill, I look at Washington, D.C.
The White House is a great thing to see
From the East Coast to the West Coast there is much beauty
Oceans and farms, mountains and valleys, cities and towns
there are so many places to be
America is the best country!

Wonderful Me
by Daniel Gutierrez

When I go to a room
And look in a mirror
I say what am I?
Then I think
I'm unique
I'm a person who likes to eat
I'm talented
I'm smart
I'm a person with a voice
I'm a person who is honest
I'm a person who cares
When I'm done thinking that
A smile appears on my face
And my day gets better
Because I am wonderful me.

Peace
by Paige Kirk

If the world was peaceful we would have the Twin Towers
Peace, that's all the world needs
If the world was peaceful we would have no wars
Peace, that's all the world needs
If the world was peaceful we would have no terrorists
Peace, that's all the world needs
If the world was peaceful no one would fight
Peace, that's all the world needs
If the world was peaceful everyone would be happy
Peace, that's all the world needs
If the world was peaceful life would always be enjoyed
Peace, that's all the world needs
If the world was peaceful we would simply, have peace
So therefore,
Peace is all we need

Tree of Life
by Saniya Harlalka

Red trees, green trees, orange trees, blue trees
They give us life
They give us care
Green leaves, orange leaves, and yellow leaves too
Filled with roots and veins
Rough branches, smooth branches, and colorful branches too
They have ridged edges and hurtful skin
But they try not to hurt us because they love us
They are the mother of nature
Let's try to conserve their beauty
Let's try not to cut their beautiful skin and majestic leaves
They fulfill our needs as much as they can
So why can't we?
Let's try to give powerful speeches about their importance
Let's try not to kill them and make this world lifeless
They give this world light and hope
Without them we are nothing
They are very helpful
So say it with me
Let's save trees!

Wind
by Haley Branflick

Whistling past ears,
Letting go of all its fears,
Sifting through the trees,
Swaying slowly like the seas.
Whispering to itself,
You might hear it yourself,
Quiet as a mouse.

Pirates
by Bryan Ouattara

Argh me matey,
It's time to get crazy.
We're going on a trip,
So, don't be lazy.
I had a dream
There is going to be another team.
We must meet them
And then defeat them.
Whoever wins
Will get the treasure.
If we win,
We will be filled with pleasure.

Mirror Me
by Hailey McDonough

Who is that over there
With glimmering yellow hair?
Shimmering eyes,
And a big bright smile!
Loves to play,
In a special way.
Wears a dress,
Here's the rest
Loves to think,
Here's what she drinks,
Water, juice, and milk.
Loves the feel of silk.
She also wears a bow.
That's me!
What do you know!

Journey
by Liam Tice

the power of pyramids and ancient skies, use that energy to make us fly
higher than clouds, past the planets, out of the galaxy and into another
fly again, high again, out and up
go up higher with the power of fire
into the corners of time and space
your journey is far from over, just over in space

Wonderful Me
by Hannah Lee

I'm wonderful when I drink
I can drink funnier than a monkey
I can make louder sounds than a lion's roar
I'm wonderful when I think
I can think more flexible than a computer
I can think faster than a robot
I'm wonderful when I talk
I can talk faster than a rapper
I can talk more emotionally than an actor
I'm wonderful when I walk
I can walk weirder than a bird
I can walk prettier than a fancy dog
I'm wonderful because only I can be me!

Spring
by Jasiah Bryant

Sun comes out bright as ever.
People go outside and smell the flowers.
Rain falls almost every day.
Inside becomes boring, outside becomes fun.
Never want the days of fun to end.
Gwen Stefani loves to sing at the end.

Forever loving smells going into your nose.
Lovable bees pollinate every day.
Over and over again, growing back.
Wonderful, joyous, soothing and amazing looks.
Everlasting they will never go away.
Rain helps them stay alive almost every day.
Sunflowers will always be my favorite flower!

Sirens
by Mia Francis

My soccer team is called the Sirens and we played a flight one team,
Everyone was dressed in colors and when we won it was like a dream.
The team was dressed in black and white,
Everyone's positions felt right.
The goalie dove to save the ball,
When we scored the ref made the call.
We ran off the field,
And as a team we all loudly squealed.

Tenaciously Endeavor To Always Succeed
by Hamzah Faisal

Tenaciously endeavor to always succeed
Tenaciously study hard to always excel
Just keep your head up high and you will be fine
Always keep fighting until you achieve all your goals
Just like how a ferocious lion fights fearlessly
It doesn't stop until it gets what it desires
If you always work hard you will get what you desire
Tenaciously endeavor to always succeed

Tiger
by Kaitlyn Martire

Black stripes zip across his body like lightning,
Orange hisses at the black
Saying he's the better color.
They fought against each other
Until they were too tired,
Finally, they laid lethargically down
And stayed there forever.
Black beady eyes scowl at his prey,
Sharp, thick nails get ready to attack,
Long, pointy teeth grin at the meal.
Wet dripping slobber drools down the carnivore's chin.
A moist, slimy nose was the one
Who scented his prey.
Suddenly, teeth clench together.
With dinner tightly secured inside his mouth,
The tiger tirelessly traipses across the terrain
With his deeply desired meal dangling
From the doorway to his stomach.

A Moment To Think
by Lindsay Inghrim

The stark darkness,
The night sedate,
The trees brusquely swaying,
The air clear of hate.
The stars scattered slovenly,
Across the clear blue sky,
The scene so very pleasing,
As it meets your eyes.
The bright red tulips,
Resting sedentary at ease,
As if they were saying
"Just leave me be please."
For people, so eager to get what they wish,
They ruin the Earth, with no thought of what happens
To the plants, or even the fish.
The exuberance of the world will be gone in a blink,
Because people won't stop for just a moment to think.

Bits of Life
by Yubin Martina Lee

Tiny magenta dots, coloring the trees
With long, thin branches, a beauty one sees
So majestic, colorful, tall, precious
Bold and beautiful, will be gone.
One by one, they fall down
Leaving our Earth, helpless.
Once a field covered with little bits of life
Is now covered in destruction.
They brought hope, light, beauty,
But not anymore. Are you going to stay there?
Not take a stand? While the life of our nature
Is withering? They tried, tried so hard
To live up to their destiny and bring us life
But now their destiny, is ruined
Because of us.
Because of us.
Now, let's live up to OUR destiny
And lend them a helping hand
Help them, help us,
Retain our little bits of life.

Broken Connection
by Jack Lemley

I dropped my phone, the dictator of my life
seeing it broken was like a deadly knife cutting through me
I was screaming like a noisy monkey
my dad called me weird but he didn't know the broken connection

Peace
by Danielle Niedosik

To have peace, we need to have a cure for autism
Look for a moment ...
You'll see everyone needs a cure
From having a disorder to not seeing
We all need a cure
We have to respect and care for each other
Life may or may not be smooth, but
We all need to be fixed like a broken toy
Peace is the cure we need.

That One Place
by Seye Magat-Carr

A boring world
A boring place
A boring world
With all the problems I don't wanna face
I'm always getting lost in all the media and gossip
Meanwhile, I don't even remember to turn off the faucet
But what if there's a place where I can escape?
A place where I'm free
Everything is not a competition or race
Where the mountains sing
And I can breathe in the fresh air from spring
Where I'll only know one thing
I won't have to worry about media or gossip or politics
I can sail all the seven seas with Captain Hix
But can you make this place come true?
Will you say there's not much we can do?
But you see no problem
It's the mind that they trick?
You think that you're healthy, but you're very very sick?
Now it's only up to you and me
Will we, together, set us all free?

Arbor Day
by Daniel Dos Santos

The trees provide fruit for the animals and humans.
Respect the trees, don't cut them, we need them to survive!
Especially made by God's hands.
Every day the trees keep us alive by giving us oxygen.
Shares shadows and homes with us and animals.

There's a Raccoon In My Bed
by Emma Kucharski

Last night I felt a fuzzball
It was squirming in my bed
I thought I felt a nibble chewing on my toe
Fighting for my bed, I fell off on my head
While he's up on my bed, I'm on the floor
Wishing I was up there I decided to stay with a fuzzball in my bed
Later that night I regret what I said
'Cause with a raccoon pulling on my covers, I had to pull them back
Last night I was fighting for my dear old cover
Much to my dismay, my covers were pulled away
My knees were pulled up to my chest
Sadly for me he decided to stay because he loves my bed

Firefighters
by Sergio Quiceno

The alarm sounds off
The men don't scoff
They slide down the pole
In the big wide hole
They jump into a truck
What they saw made them horror-struck
A building on fire
Roaring like a town crier
The water sprays
But the fire dances and plays
The battle rages
It seems like ages
The spraying comes to a close
And the fire just glows
The fire is out
The firemen shout

The Perfect Snow Day
by Samantha Mancuso

I jumped out of bed
AHH! It's snowing
I want to sled
Because the wind is blowing
The trees are so white
With fluffy snow
That makes them bright
To make them show
The sun is peeking out
It was so awesome
I started to shout
Because I saw a possum
I had such a long day
I wish there were more
It was the perfect snow day
And I couldn't ask for more

Why Do Things Have To Happen?
by Cate Riely

Why do things have to happen?
Why does the Earth have to orbit the sun?
Why does war have to kill?
But of all the whys in the world,
Why does our school have to close?
This was my home,
this was my refuge ,
This was where I was meant to be,
But all good things have to go away,
Like a flower in the spring,
eventually it will wither in summer's great heat,
Alas this school is like a nest
High up in the trees,
Safe from all predators
But when that nest breaks,
the baby birds get tossed out in the world
Knowing they might never come back to their old life …

Why?
by Annika Storer

Why do we have to fight?
Why can't we be happy together?
Why do we have so much anger?
Why do we yell?
Why do we cry?
Why don't we have peace in the world?
Why?

Peace
by Elizabeth Hjorth

They have the essence of light
Yet they're not unicorns or fairies
They may make you scream
But you have to accept them
Different pots
Different people
Gerbils and rats
Dogs and cats
Respect all likes
And it all leads to peace

My Favorite Things
by Patrick Bush

I am crazy about funny Smosh videos.
I especially love experimenting because it is fun.
I like Tyler. He is entertaining.
I live to play "Just Dance" and have "Happy" feet.
My favorite dinner is sweet, squishy steamers.
Warm cheesy pizza really makes my day.
I dream or hope to be a famous dancer.
I am thankful for my grandma.
I am passionate about motocross.
I am excited when I see a shiny dirt bike.
Envious when I smell dirt bike exhaust
and jubilant when I hear the roar of an engine.
These are a few of my favorite things!
When I have a lot of chores,
When I get in trouble,
I remember a few of my favorite things, and then I feel happy again!

Happy Birthday
by Sam Grube

It's your birthday today
Let's go and play
There is no delay
We'll have cake, "Hooray!"
Now I think it's time to say,
"Happy Birthday!"

Winter
by Isabella No

I feel the wind against my cheek
I hear the birds honk with their beak
I smell the coolness of winter
I also smell the burning timber
I see the clouds sparkling white
To me it really is a beautiful sight

Cancun
by Kaylee Park

Cancun, oh Cancun,
How I love you so.
I hope to see you soon.
On a plane, I will go.
We wake up super early with a sigh,
To catch our flight.
I say my good-byes,
Until he is out of sight.
We check into our hotel,
While looking at the tags,
With many stories to tell,
As we get out tagged bags.
If you're getting kind of lazy
Just order room service
Instead of getting crazy,
Or really, really nervous.
Cancun is the best!
With chicken wings by my side,
On a lounge chair I rest
As I open my mouth wide.

A Meal and Some Fun
by Ryan Cekic

One chicken,
Two plates, four forks, five knives,
Six spoons at lunch.
One, two, three, four, five balls for play.
Good day.

Peace
by Jack VanOrden

Stop war
Please stop
Make the world better
Just stop war
Believe
If you believe, anything can happen
The world is in our hands
Don't let it slip away
We are destroying the world
Just stop

My Hero
by Joshua Justin

He is a hero in many ways.
He looks after us during the night and during the day.
He inspires us to be better, to look out for one another, to always stay together.
He words hard and studies harder.
He believes knowledge will always take you farther.
He goes to all my tournaments and all my games.
If he's not in the stands it's just not the same.
He makes us study but also makes us laugh.
He even taught us how to take a bath.
He taught us how to tie our shoes and fold our pants.
When we cross the street he holds our hand.
When I grow up I want to be just like him.
The days will be brighter and the moon will dim.
He makes us happy when we are sad.
The man I'm writing about is my dad.

A Spectacular Season
by Charles Ehrsam

Sunny the whole time
Unlimited times to play
Most fun out of all the seasons
Many activities to do
Extra ice cream to eat
Really cool places to go

Peace
by Alissa Arabia

Stop fighting
For a second
Solve your problems
Be nice to all people
No matter how different you are
Work together like ants in a colony
Stop shouting out
Think before you speak

The Adventures of Fall
by Kaitlyn Acevedo

When it's the end of September,
I start to remember.
Birds start to fly south,
In search of food to fill their mouth.
Pumpkin picking is fun,
Until it's all said and done.
Red, yellow, and brown leaves on the ground,
I stand to jump and play in the mound.
When the wind carries the leaves away,
There is nothing more I can say.
As darkness gets longer
Fall starts to grow stronger.
Thanksgiving dinner on the table,
Fall starts to become unstable.
The temperature gets colder,
Fall becomes less bolder.
The first frost glistens on the ground,
The ground that has already browned.
Fall has finally left,
As winter sneaks in with her deft.

Food
by Marcus Respicio

Eat food,
Some are healthy.
I like to eat pizza.
It is very nice and crispy
Tastes good.

Easter Preparations
by Nicole Okur

Easter is a special day where Jesus rose from His lay.
He died for us to save us from sin, he fought with Satan and had a win.
The Triduum includes three special days, we celebrate them in amazing ways.
Holy Thursday is how we start, Jesus washed feet to show His heart.
Good Friday is the next day, we celebrate it in a different way.
Jesus had just died, many people had cried.
Holy Saturday is a special day, we pray, and pray, and pray.
It is now Easter Sunday and Christ has risen!

The Amazing United States
by Hailey Singer

They fled in masses across the vast sea
In order to escape and be free
They were sick and tired of religious persecution
Finding a new land to live in would be the solution
They came without money, all they had was what they could carry
They came to this land to prosper and to marry
When I sit in my house reading, writing, and practicing however I please
I cannot help but think that someone sacrificed it all for me
Our country is full of opportunity, I could grow up and be whatever I want to be
A teacher, a lawyer, even the president of our great country
I know with hard work I could go from rags to riches
And accomplish all that I have set out, my hopes and my wishes
We are so lucky our country is fair and just
With three branches, checks and balances, we can trust
I'm always so proud my voice will be respected
When we exercise our right to vote our officials will be elected
What makes America so special is not only its rights and privileges
But its states, cities, counties and villages
Its citizens come from near and far, all genders, religion, color and race
All these things together make up one amazing United States

Flowers
by Paige Iino

Flowers, flowers all kinds of flowers
More will bloom on April showers
Flowers, flowers all kinds of colors
Red ones, white ones, and even bright ones as summer
Flowers, flowers all kinds of shapes
Heart shapes, diamond shapes, and even pie cakes
So as you walk, take a good look
Stems of flowers that are shaped like hooks

Peace
by Stephanie Haessig

To be understanding
To stop, just stop
Stop and smell the roses
We shall open up our hearts and sing
Sing a song
Sing a love song
We shall pray for no more wars
Pray for families to be in peace
And never fight
For our parents to never fight

I Am Poem: My Favorite Things
by Nolan Kinkead

I am crazy about crazy, mazy, hazy Christmas.
I especially love airplanes because I feel like a bird.
I like Dad. He cooks really well.
I live to play soccer, running and relaxing
My favorite snack is a brownie. It is fluffy, chocolaty, and delicious!
Nutella cupcakes can really make my day!
I dream or hope to build a boat.
I am thankful for my house.
I am passionate about having fun tubing.
I am vicious when I see caramel candy.
Delighted when I smell flowers and excited when I hear the bell at school.
These are a few of my favorite things!
When I am down, when I feel like crying,
I remember a few of my favorite things, and then I am empowered!

Arbor Day
by Kaya Lancaster

Arbor Day is when we celebrate our trees!
Recycle to preserve our trees.
Branches give many animals homes.
Our trees give us the oxygen we need to breathe.
Really fun leaf piles, nice shade, and fruit.

Dangerous fires have destroyed many forests.
And buildings are taking away our trees too.
You should plant a tree on this day!

Life
by Holden Crouthamel

Life is something you enjoy
Like playing with Joey
You can have so much fun
Life is never done
If you do not like how you live
Then just find a new life and live
Life brings good and bad things
The bad and good things in life are what make life
You have a life, I have a life
This is life

Peace
by Emily Shields

No fighting in life
You need to respect others
And treat others the way you want to be treated
For respect back
Be friendly and kind
And we can get peace
To give and to get back
Peace, love, and kindness
We need to be those things
To make a beautiful country
We need to love each other
To depend on each other
To have each others' backs
And that is how we can find peace

Peace
by Mark Yosco

If we could respect others and be thoughtful
If everyone would just be helpful and help each other
Be caring and loving to others
We need to be helpful and make this world happy
If everyone would be kind and not fight
Peace

Nature
by Kelsey Villareal

See the flowers
blooming
trees growing
and
the sun blazing
with light.
All the creatures
come out
and wander about.
Oh, how beautiful
and
wonderful nature
is!

Pool With the Bees
by Ava Gonzalez

I go to the pool
To sit on the bench.
Don't bring your tools,
Or they will get drenched.
When I sit, it is very sunny,
But then I see a bee.
I think it might want some honey.
So then, I try to grab my car keys.
When I find them, I get in the car.
I had honey that I bought with my money.
It was in a jar.
I wish instead of bees, I saw a bunny.
So then, I throw the honey and drive away.
I want to go home.
Then, I think this is what must happen in May.

A Recipe For Peace
by Quinn Kiessling

12 cups of apology
1 cup of chocolate hugs
Dash of order
Cup of friends
Love sauce
Mix together
Cook
Eat

Fly
by Taylor Fallon

When the dragons get up to fly
They'll go up into the sky
And when they get tired they'll fall
It won't take long because they're tall
When it is night, they will fight
fight for food that is
And in the morning it will be hard
they will go hunt for food
In the sky
They will fly high
Until the end.

Cake!
by Katelyn Pezeur

Life is good
Life is great
Now eat some chocolate cake!
Eat it up
Until you're stuffed
Then make some more!
Pour some milk
Wrap it in silk
For it is a present
Now isn't that pleasant?
Give it to someone
And that someone is you!
Eat your cake
And celebrate too!

Showers and Flowers
by Phoebe Costalos

Spring is my favorite season,
And I love it for a reason.
My family spends time together,
Because we have beautiful weather.
Spring has lovely trees,
But my favorite is the breeze.
I can play sports,
Without doing many reports.
Spring will come to an end,
But summer will bring a new friend.

Friendships
by Jada Davis

Funny jokes
Reliable friends
Interesting conversation
Embarrassing moments
Never-ending companionship
Devoted companion for life
Secret keeping
Hugs and love forever
Impossible separation
Plenty of forgiveness
Successful lives together

Please Don't Give Us Extra Homework Tonight
by Bisan Allan

Please don't give us extra homework tonight we promise we'll behave.
Please don't give us extra homework tonight the exterminator is coming today.
Please don't give us extra homework I just know we can be good,
please don't give us extra homework I'm going to watch *Robin Hood*.
Please don't give us extra homework I really hate to complain,
please don't give us extra homework I'm really in a great deal of pain.
Please don't give us extra homework tonight I'd hate to scream and cry,
please don't give us extra homework there is a new game on Gamefly.
Okay, no homework for you instead go home and do the excuses you've used
and then write a report titled as ... ha-ha that's homework for you!

Baseball
by Noah Kang

One ball,
Two outs, one strike,
Six wooden bats, six gloves.
One runs, slides and makes a home run!
Great job!

Zootopia
by Katarzyna Petelski

Zootopia
Watching prey and predator live together
Sweet!
Then everything changed
Predators went nuts
Nobody knew why
Judy and the other officers had to find
Out what was going on
At the end, it was a syndrome
That drove them crazy
Bad Sheep
Bellwether
Until order was restored

Marshmallow Trip
by Minji Kang

There was a cow.
He liked everything that was sweet.
One day, a cow found some marshmallows.
He thought it was raw meat.
So, he brought it to his friend, Cat.
He thought Cat could eat raw meat.
She at it and said, "It's better than a rat."
Then, the cow said he bought it on the street.
Cow and Cat put on their shoes.
They went to Smart Owl's house to ask what kind of meat they would eat.
Owl said, "I really don't have a clue."
Then, they met a mouse.
They showed the mouse the meat they would eat.
The mouse said, "It's not meat!
It's marshmallows."

Waves
by Richard Andres Gonzalez

Waves are blue and skies are blue
do you know that I love dolphins too
they're blue
so you can't see them very good

Morning
by Jacob Linder

Birds singing their morning songs.
Squirrels bolting up trees.
Deer hiding among the branches.
The moon tucking itself into bed.
The sun awaking nature,
Dressing the trees.
Get ready for a new day, a new you, a new world.

Weird
by Jessica Grissett

I am weird

Wonderful
Exciting
Interesting
Real
Different

I am weird
laugh, love
kind, trust
the things
I am are
buried in
my soul
tell the stories
that were
never told I
love that
life is a gift.
I'll never give
up on this
wish.

Who Knows?
by Nelson Clermont

Who knows when our parents are going to win the lottery?
Who know when the earth is going to stop spinning?
Who knows what's going to happen in infinity years?
Who knows how future cars are going to look?
Who knows when we are going to see Mary? God?
Who knows when there will be peace in our world?
Who knows? Who knows?

What We Do On Mondays
by Zoe Laffler

Our bikes' wheels are as circular as a doughnut, and as fast as a race car.
We ride down the sidewalks, riding all through downtown.
We stop every now and then, to buy some penny candy.
Then we go, to the tree fort.
We open up the library.
Sometimes it's six or seven of us kids, big kids and little kids too.
People says it's like a movie, but that's just what we do.
That's what we do on Mondays.

Kingdom of God
by Dena Mistichelli

As I went to go read a book under a tree in the park,
I started thinking about God And how I love him so much
He is the creator of the Earth
God is a forgiver and always fulfills his promises
He has a soft, calming voice, a warming smile, and a great heart
He is peaceful and sacrificing
God is like a vine and we are the branches
God is like a boomerang he always comes back to us after we sin
God is as graceful as a dove flying in the bright sky
God is peaceful; he is a dove
God is a vine, he gives us fruit
After I think I start to get up and take a stroll
As I walk I can see trees as tall as a skyscraper
The leaves are a big as my face
As I stared at the hug tree the vines wrap me in a hug
The vine finally let go of me and I walked all the way home
When I get home I sit in my room and say out loud to myself
God loves everyone equally
I will never forget that

3rd Place

Grace Davis

Ode To Change
by Grace Davis

My fickle companion pulls me forward
through a rolling, spinning mess.
You can be as cold as a blizzard's wind,
or as warm as a mother's caress.
You wipe your paintbrush of insecurity
across my canvas heart.
Until a masterpiece of character is revealed,
and you, Change, set me apart.
You gift some with the strength of heroes,
but send others to their knees.
You bring about an outcome,
that at first no eye sees.
Like a tapestry of emotions,
you weave through someone's life.
Strands of love, hope, and joy
mixed with fear, loneliness, and strife.
My life you rearrange.
I love and hate you, Change.

Isabel Yates

Property
by Isabel Yates

They killed my father
Whipped him with a whip of hatred.
Slapped him with the slap of a thousand tears.
I could no longer bear the pain.
I ran.
I thought I was safe but I was caught
thrown into prison like a useless rag doll
left to rot until my future was decided.
I'd be branded and left in the stocks
it didn't matter, nothing mattered anymore.
I lingered in the stocks
watching the brand warming in the skillet
preparing for the satisfying taste of my burnt flesh.
The brand bites into my cheek
melting my flesh
blurring my vision
a wildfire of pain rages through me.
Clinging to my soul, shredding my heart
but leaving its mark
P for Property.

1st Place

Gabriella Wang

Gabriella writes to us as a fourth grade student who,
in addition to being an award winning author,
is also an accomplished violinist, singer, dancer, and actor
with a special love for musical theater.
When she's not playing with her two cats,
you may find her on horseback,
as she also enjoys riding competitions.
Excellent work, Gabriella!

Flame Tiger
by Gabriella Wang

You clutch the matchbox in your hand,
And poise it at the ready.
The spindly wooden stick advances,
You flick your wrist just so.
With it comes that stealthy sound,
And springing from a winter's sleep,
The flame tiger arises.
He reaches out with sneaky paws
To grab at candles passing by.
His tail creeps across the match,
Then you hastily blow him off
And send him to his bedroom.
"You've done your job, and now it's time
For you to take your nap."
His essence lingers in the air,
And leaves some smoky paw prints.

62   *Accomplished*

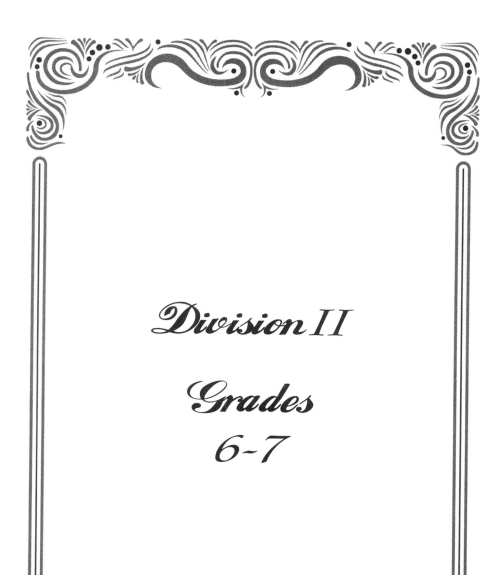

Division II

Grades
6-7

Tornado's Destruction
by Avril Selah

Spinning rapidly, around and around,
In a constant funnel of destruction,
Disintegrating anything in its wake,
One of Mother Nature's deadliest forces.
Winds howling,
Houses dancing,
Trees conversing upon themselves,
People trying to cope with the wind.
Thousands mourned,
Tremendous amounts of people dead,
Just as many homes devastated.
But as time went on,
We helped rebuild our community,
Piece by piece,
Helping our community become strong again.

Neverland
by Alana Muller

Peter Pan, Peter Pan, please take me to Neverland.
Show me all the magic you can do and show me all the creatures too.
Neverland, Neverland where you never have to grow up.
Run freely through the magical meadows
where your mind will glow with thoughts of rainbows.
Peter Pan, Peter Pan, please take me to Neverland.

Bald Eagle
by Luis Baum

Our country's Bald Eagle
Stronger than any other bird
Fighting strong in battle
Sharing our country's freedom
Stronger than any other bird
Soaring high in the sky
Sharing our country's freedom
Flying at our side
Soaring high in the sky
Fighting strong in battle
Flying at our side
Our country's Bald Eagle

Without You
by Adriana Santos

Alone I waited in the rain
Memories filled with much sorrow and pain
And so my happiness and joy went down the drain
Tears ran down my cheeks
Like a hundred fast flowing creeks
And I could barely speak
To the sound of thunder
I did much wonder
About my loving mother
I sit here now with no hand to hold
My hair turning grey and I'm getting old
The light at the end of the tunnel has claimed my soul

Morals Have No Ends
by Catherine Antonelli

I brood over the concept of free will each day.
Yet what no individual has the capacity to discern is the morality
of the dog sauntering in their backyard.
It must feed and reproduce and drink and slumber.
Conceivably: it knows not of genuine altruism; it is an egoist.
If it loves you, it will safeguard you, but such love is only a visceral
means of survival.
In the chasms of its soul is a dog grappling its adversary
in the soils of the woods,
its vocal chords thundering in vehement acrimony.
It savagely thrusts its teeth into the scruff of a fellow dog
and wrests the skin from its body with the potency of a panther,
watching it perish. The victor urinates on the now-owned sod;
at last, prey is profuse. It must survive– so it disavows morals!
And no one discerns the ant boring the earth beneath them–
the conscientious conventionalist.
A dutiful, punctilious collectivist that labors ponderously and dies
in its grueling social authoritarianism ... yet nonetheless sustains its existence.
Truthfully, both extremes are repugnant and exhort humanity further into the
tenebrous, languid arms of death. Either we are too exploitative or daft;
too hedonistic or dutiful ... Such antitheses are only derived from animals,
as they were never acquainted with morality, only their one common
desideratum: survival.
Thus, if every action is only the means to an iniquitous yet imperative end,
I surmise with earnest melancholia that there is no free will–
or simply no morality …

I Am
by Jordan Dasher

I am smart and funny.
I wonder if I can achieve my dream.
I hear a shriek.
I see superheroes.
I want video games.
I am smart and funny.
I pretend to have powers.
I feel happiness.
I touch upon life.
I worry about my grades.
I cry about stuff that annoys me.
I am smart and funny.
I understand math.
I say to try your best.
I dream that I can fly.
I try at video games.
I hope to achieve in life.
I am smart and funny.

Faith
by Juliana Carrillo

She was in a wheelchair and couldn't walk.
She was deaf and couldn't talk.
She was blind and couldn't see.
Sometimes I think that girl is me.
She cries every night.
She wishes she had a sight.
She falls on her knees.
Sometimes I think that girl is me.
She falls down,
And makes a frown.
She tries to get back up,
And she didn't know she was grabbing onto her pup.
This time she stands,
She thought she was in fairyland.
This time she sees,
She thought it was just in her dreams.
This time she said her first word,
And she heard herself say it in the wrong order.
Now she wants to move on,
And enjoy life and be gone.

Proud To Be Me
by Alexa Lucius

I am smart and caring.
I wonder what will happen to me in the future.
I hear children crying.
I see myself taking care of kids in the future.
I want to become a pediatrician.
I am smart and caring.
I pretend that one day I will become one of the most famous pediatricians ever.
I feel great when I help kids and other people.
I touch a person's chest to feel their heartbeat.
I worry that I cannot cure a child's sickness.
I am smart and caring.
I understand why children cry in a doctor's office
I say that you can accomplish your goal if you work hard and study.
I dream that I cured all children's diseases.
I try to study as hard as I can.
I hope I can make my dad and mom proud of me.
I am smart and caring.

Stormy Night of the Twister
by Jonathan Campbell

It was a stormy night
when the end came.
Without any sunlight
only the sky was to blame.
It whirled and swirled
with no sign of stopping.
The twister was whopping.
The wind was roaring,
and the rain was pouring.
We took shelter,
to wait out the welter.
When it finally ended
the result was all but splendid.
Damaged and destroyed,
demolished and devoid.
But it's not our ends,
as it brings us together as friends.
To rebuild and reshape
our broken landscape.

Why Am I Not Tall?
by Christopher Faringthon

Why am I not a skyscraper,
Like my best of friends?
Why am I not taller,
Than a mere sixth grader?
Is it because I have,
A hobbit of a father?
Is it due to the lack,
Of sports I play?
Is it only because,
I haven't hit my growth
Spurt yet?
Or am I just meant to,
Be like this?

The Red Lady
by Ishita Jadon

She walks in beauty.
Masked in mystery.
Burning brightly in a brilliant blaze.
Powerful, graceful, prominent, and gracious.
The fire burns and spreads.
She is cloaked in flowing silk the color of a living flame.
She twirls and turns, swoops and spins, skipping playfully on thin air.
She showers the park with royal red sparks.
Kissing the ground on her delicate red shoes.
She sends sheets of flames, leaping and curling.
The fire burns and spreads.
Then she leaves with a silent blessing.
Black snow lingering in the shimmering fiery air.
Just a willowy figure standing in the light,
mahogany hair floating freely in the wind.
An angel of destruction.
-Found Poem Sources Attributed To:
"She Walks In Beauty" by Lord Byron
Horoscope.com
"Ash and Bramble" by Sarah Prineas
Rose Marie Cortenga, Laredo, TX, "The Azrael Project"
"Those Other Days" by Edward Phillips Oppenheim
"Pirates, Ghosts, and Coastal Lore: The Best of Judge Whedbee"
by Charles Harry Whedbee

Everyone Has a Desire
by Ivan Lam

Everyone has a desire
May it be winning the lottery or not
It will burn like fire
It will affect you for the rest of your life
Even as you retire
Everyone has a desire

The Firefly Path
by Diana Mendoza

Lost in darkness
With hearts so hollow
The fireflies are creating
a path to follow
Although we might feel alone
We must not lose hope
For on this night
under their watchful light
They will show us
The way back home

He Who Came
by Christina DelQuaglio

He was tap-dancing on the roof
and blowing through the trees,
he walked through all the houses
not caring about me.
I thought about my life,
I wanted to flee,
but where can I go
I'm without my family.
I clenched what was nearby
I held on tight,
hoping I would be able
to get through the night.
I wondered and believed,
I hoped and I prayed,
and it all came true
when I woke up to a sunny day.
He finally liked me, he finally cared.

Paper
by Sphia Sadek

marks are written on it
every day
drawings, math, writing pieces, art are what you will
find
made by trees, and is a shade of
white
paper lets you to express
anything.
and one of the things is this
poem.

Epic Fail At the Pool
by Alyssa Fuentes

I knew from the moment I saw him,
I knew that it was love.
I saw him at a swim meet,
It's like he came from above.
Passionate and fierce when competing,
But also caring and kind to those he beats.
Alas, our paths will never cross
As we are never in the same heat.

The Evil Hurricane
by Angela Russo

Wind howled through the night sky, it pounded against homes.
Residents were awakened from their beauty sleep.
Droplets of rain came falling from the sky,
the rain washed away the city until it was squeaky clean.
Sadly, some people were eaten by the storm,
others luckily got spit out.
Pieces of debris floated in what used to be roads,
but now serves as a river that transports leftover trash.
Although, trash was treasure.
Photos, china, and jewelry from the community's homes swam along the streets
People salvaged through the knee-deep water on the hunt for their prized possessions
The rain masked tears that tumbled down the cheeks of many.
Muggy water covered up the pretty features of the town
where fresh flowers used to line the sidewalks.
Now, moving forward is the only option.

Life Is Fun
by Ben Bratter

Life is fun, when you play in the sun,
You play with friends, but then it ends,
Like the sun at night, it is a remembered sight,
Your heart is sad, a memory had,
Never cry, everything has to die.

Footprint
by Charlotte Oliver

None, not even us
Can know what will come from these
It's our mark we leave
It's how we inspire
After the day we are gone
The only thing we have left
Is what we have done
By the next morning rise
Will we be conscious
Vision is blinded
When apprehension takes over
We must know of we

Littering
by Tolu Adesanya

The trash falls and hits the ground
Nowhere to be found
Hidden behind the can
It should have fallen in
People pass it day by day
It looks at the ground in dismay
No one stops to pick it up
Finally it's had enough
The wind blows and pushes it forward
Finally it can be heard
A person comes and sees it there
And it gives them a bit of a scare
They pick it up and stare again
Then put it in the trash can
Finally surrounded by all its friends
This piece of trash has a happy end!

The Tall Building
by Angelie Chitre

a building so
tall
high in the
sky
looks upon everyone
near
while protecting those
inside.

Nobody But You
by Janee Gravenhise

The people that I trusted in life
From the time I was born until now
Was nobody but you
Then you broke that trust
Faster than the speed of light
And the people in my life who ruined it
Was nobody but you
Now I have learned my lesson
That no one can be trusted
That I have to trust myself
I still don't trust anybody
Including you

Solution To Saving the Earth
by Janai Campbell

When you take care of trees.
You will be pollution free.
To take care of pollution.
I have a simple solution.
Recycling is good for the environment.
Helping should be a requirement.
We need to start recycling.
We can simply do this by bicycling.
Mix up your leftovers to make compost.
This will help the environment the most.
We can make this place a better land.
If everyone gives a helping hand.

A Bitter Life
by Emma Freire

Branches that sway on me,
Garbage lays at my feet.
Plastic bags in the air,
Still there is garbage down there.
People try to clean me up,
But still there is no luck.
Garbage here, garbage there,
People litter everywhere.
Littering is bad it's no good,
Please help I live in your neighborhood.
Up so high I could touch the sky,
If you don't stop, then I will die.
If I die a lot will be lost,
There is nothing to replace the cost.
Trees are something the world doesn't consider,
But without me the world would be bitter!

Childish Whims
by Sophia Carter

Under the fierce control of impulse and ad campaigns,
You find yourself in a store
Reaching for an object-
A toy that simply enraptured you when you first spotted it.
It fits perfectly into the life you've pictured for yourself ...
But deep down you know better.
Satisfaction!
It's all you begged,
Even pleaded for,
When you first
Tore and wrung out
The contents of your wallet.
But the satisfaction; the "happiness" only lasts as long
As a wave upon the sand.
For the moment it has engulfed each grain of you in its cool bliss,
It is slowly,
Painfully
Dragged away.
It promises only to return if you can succumb to another passing fancy-
Another childish whim.

The Beauty of Earth
by Brea Henderson

We only have one Earth
We need to treasure what it's worth
Read this poem and you will see
Earth's amazing beauty
You see and feel the big, warm sun
And feeling breezes is fun
The rich soil and amazing plants
And the animals from birds to ants
Bodies of water from oceans to lakes
Filled with lots of fish and snakes
The joy of nature is a blessing
But watching it get wasted is stressing
Reduce, reuse and recycle
Every day go through this cycle
You will be happier now and then
When you find nature is your friend

Invisible Me
by Catarina Guimaraes

People around me
Can they see
I try to get their attention
But I want to run and flee
If only they saw
Not invisible me
But my transparent body
Couldn't fool a bee
Do they know how I feel
That I'm hurting inside
That invisible me
has something to hide
I put a smile on my face
And right before noon
Invisible me's
Heart breaks so soon
A fragile heart and body
That invisible me holds
My only wish
To be strong and bold

Destruction of My Youth
by Jason Laderas

The destruction of my youth
In front of my eyes
I can't stop it now, I shouldn't even try
My sandcastles have been destroyed
"Bob the Builder" is gone
"Max and Ruby" has ran its race
These new dances make me wanna cry
Silentó brings tears to my eyes
The "Nae-Nae" makes me cringe
The "Whip" makes me die
And if you're wondering
Yes, it is too late to say sorry
The destruction of my youth
In front of my eyes
I can't stop it now, I shouldn't even try
R.I.P. my youth

Earthquakes
by Maryssa Mills

It all began normally,
A completely normal day.
It was normal as normal could be,
So what came next was unexpected.
The floors began to rumble,
The furniture shook,
The lights knocked against one another.
I looked up from my homework,
My chair moving underneath me.
My parents stood as still as stones,
Each of us afraid to move.
Sounds of glasses crashing from the tables to the floors,
There goes my mother's expensive pottery.
Books clattered against the shelves,
Tumbling to the ground.
Like it had begun,
It stopped.
So suddenly, I could not comprehend.
I sat still on my stool,
The only chair that had not fallen.

Save the Earth
by Kayla Riley

Pollution is bad for the Earth
But what is it really worth
Pollution can harm the air
And it seems like nobody really cares
Recycling can reduce pollution
There are many green resolutions
Conserving energy will also help
And the results will make someone joyously yelp
Wildlife can also be effected greatly
Have you heard how many animals have died lately?
The Earth's people should plant more trees
Which would probably be inhabited by many bees
We can save the Earth any day
And make the Earth happy and gay
Picking up trash is one way
To stop pollution today

Huang River Floods
by Jeffrey Min

The rain came down heavy,
like the tears of Heaven,
sorry about what it would do.
The river rises,
it rises up angry,
angry at all the trash
and people that dirtied it.
It sweeps across the towns.
And stays.
2 dead,
4 dead,
7 dead,
37 dead.
The water continues to rise.
134, 3,700,000 dead,
buildings start to capsize.
Disease and despair spread through China.
Then slowly, the waters recede.
The flood was gone.
But wait, did I misread?
There was another, and another!
The Yellow River would bleed China's people dry.

I Am
by Rachel Arauz

I am proud and sweet.
I wonder about stars and moons.
I hear dogs barking.
I see dinosaurs on schools.
I want to go on a roller skating field trip.
I am proud and sweet.
I pretend my friends are dinosaurs.
I feel surprised or excited.
I touch or l touch monsters.
I worry about the animals.
I cry about the doctor flu shot.
I am proud and sweet.
I understand what my teachers try to say.
I say thunderstorms.
I dream about my friends.
I try to do a math addition.
I hope to be a rock star.
I am proud and sweet.

There Was a Time
by Malaika Ezetah

There was a time when people sang
Joined together as one
With connections deeper than the depths of the ocean.
There was a time when people danced
Using beautiful expression as a passageway
To another's soul.
There was a time when people lived
When they sought the fascinating.
The beautiful. The wondrous.
And they found that within each other.
The fascinating that is one's relationship with another.
The beauty that love and compassion bring to the table.
The wondrous and complex, human connections.,
They found it.
People no longer sing
They no longer join together with powerful words
People no longer dance
For expression of one's feelings
People no longer live
But they need to, now more than ever

Winter
by McKenna Holz

It was freezing cold outside.
The lack of warmth was extraordinary.
The frost on the windows were like
Intricate puzzle pieces fitting together.
Winter had arrived.
She didn't stop blowing
On the trees.
Nor did she stop freezing
The shimmering ponds.
She can be as destructive,
Or as peaceful as she wants.
Winter has complete control
Over the weather.
And she wants cold, snowy temperatures.
But I have a feeling it will be a warm winter
This year.
She is my best friend after all,
Even though we are polar opposites.

His Smile
by Jenna Weisbach

The golden ray of sun spreads upon his face
And as he starts to smile it picks up pace
It spreads to me and I smile widely
He hugs me close and holds me kindly
And over the years he did the same
As the clock ticked counting down the hours till I came
Home from a long day
Every time I'd see him I'd smile
I'd look at him and be happy for a while
But then one day one rainy day
I was told he would not stay
That his smile would go away
And so would the way
He hugged me each day
He would be gone
For very long
And the people wept
As the memories that were kept
Were shared
And the family and friends stayed close as they shared
memories of my grandpa and his smile

Pictures
by Priscilla Rampersad

Pictures stop time,
Not just used to solve a crime.
Pictures capture a single moment,
Not to rewind and play it again.
Pictures bring tears, not sorrows.
Pictures show but a time and place
Just to bring you back face to face,
Not to show you what was,
but what could have been.
Pictures stop time,
They bring you back to a place of mind.
They rewind what is lost and gone,
They bring tears filled with new fears.
You soon realize, face to face:
Pictures are the best place.
- In memory of David Bhola

I Have Been Afraid
by Aaron Wesley Saunders

Everything has a story,
Or history one could say,
But everything must end,
For its name to stay,
I have been afraid,
Afraid of many things,
they're dangling in my heart,
From a long thin string,
If something doesn't end,
Then what was its purpose or meaning?
If something doesn't end,
Then that thing becomes demeaning,
Every great thing has to have an "end of the line",
Like it or not there will always be an end of time,
Whether the time comes early,
Or the time comes late,
There will always be a reason to conceal something's fate,
I have been afraid,
Afraid of many things,
Those things are dangling in my heart,
From a long thin string,
My fears will one day end, long before I do,
Everything must die, even fears too.

Soldiers
by Ethan Richards

Thud! Blackness
A strange phenomenon, the glistening sun
Divine beams of light ablaze
A mystifying aurora
In the marvelous haze
I hear men laughing
In a magnificent perspective
Making an alliance of unity
Where all is well and peace is an objective
I wake up to the sound of gunshots
And hot explosions of blazing flame
A grisly view
A bloody shame
I hear men screaming
In this ugly setting
Afflicting pain and suffering to others
This war is terrible and I won't soon be forgetting

Homework
by Tiara Jenkins

Homework is the worst thing ever!
When you do it, it takes forever.
In social studies, all you need to know
Are things that happened long ago.
Like Christopher Columbus sailed the ocean blue
Somewhere around 1492.
In science, it's a lot of fun things to learn and see.
We get to mix chemicals and learn chemistry.
But, when it comes to difficult questions,
Just leave me out of the discussion.
I don't even want to mention math
Because there are so many different paths.
Language arts is the best part.
It has been from the start.
I have the best teacher, Mr. Cieradkowski.
He likes to surf out in the blue sea.
But when I have a 6 paragraph essay I have to write,
I really hope I can get sleep tonight.
Even though I don't want to learn stuff like slope or dilation,
I still have to get my education.

Never
by Wynzel Geronimo

Shattered windows
Part of a broken tree
A fallen skyscraper,
Being rebuilt
A daffodil in a field of roses
Aiming high
For the sky
Always seems to crash back down

Broken
by Henrique Teixeira

You have taken
My love
That laid
In my heart
And which
You were probably
Giving to
Another being
I will not
Forgive you
This time
I am too broken.

I Don't Think I Am a Musician
by Layla Pluhowski

I do not think I am a musician
Sure my fingers play the keys
And my foot taps to the beat
And I memorize the music
And hum along to the song.
But I'd rather be
Stuffing my nose in a book
And daydreaming about fictional worlds
And imagining impossible scenarios
And reading about made-up places.
And listening to someone else's music
I don't think I'm a musician.

The Goodbye, My Friend
by Khushi Patel

Walking alone through the street
Everything was thumping just like my heartbeat
Wild people looking around
Out of nowhere someone threw me to the ground
Calling aloud
Someone echoed out loud
Jumping in fear
Nothing seemed clear
I knew everything came to an end
Knowing I didn't even have a friend
To hold and trust
Since they saw me in such disgust
Ending my life
someone please pass the knife
Oh darlin'
goodbye …

Problems With Paper
by Melissa Somwaru

A man once looked at a piece of paper.
He said there are many problems with this piece of paper.
I wondered to myself if this man was crazy.
For what can one piece of paper do to you.
The man continued and said,
"How would you like to be hurt by paper?"
I thought about his question thinking of a paper cut,
But when the man spoke, I was far from right.
"A paper will have words,
And it's the words that hurt you.
The paper gives the words,
The opportunity to hurt you."
The old man spoke, the old man was right.
Words can hurt you all day, words can hurt you all night.
However, is the paper at fault, for the hurtful words?
The man responded,
"Yes, for if there was no paper, there would be no words."
I thought about this for a long while.
How can there be a problem,
With something as plain as paper?

He Broke Me
by Sara Marin

The words that he said broke me
It was like I was frozen in place screaming inside
heartbreak was one thing I was supposed to hide
knowing there was nothing I could do
the only thing that broke me was you
I could feel the tears coming, knowing I couldn't be strong
While you thought there was nothing wrong.
He broke me again, nothing was the same
He was the player, I was the game
He said he loved me, while he was looking at another
like I lost a child and I was the mother
You take pictures of things you don't want to lose
You were an artist, but I wasn't your muse
First I was excited
then I was depressed
you burned something that was never ignited
My demons came back stronger than ever
what was once forever is now never, he broke me

I Am a Girl
by Kelise Smith

I am a girl
With a mom who doesn't care
I am a girl
Who doesn't know how to brush her hair
I am a girl
Who can't get a date
I am a girl
That has to face her fate
I am a girl
I have feelings and emotions
I am a girl
My tears make oceans
I am a girl
My friend likes to visit
I am a girl
I never once missed it
I am a girl
That's it
I'm a girl
And here in my world
I am nothing but a girl

The Cat and the Rat
by Maura Downing

Yesterday I saw a cat,
Lying on a mat
While singing to his bat,
He saw a rat
Screaming while he sat,
The cat killed the rat
"I now have a hat!"
Said the cat

Friends That Care
by Jade Rose Martorano

The ones that pick you up when you fall down
The ones that support what you say
Who stays close to you and never gives you a frown
Who makes sure you're okay all day
Who makes you laugh
Who makes you feel good
Who splits time in half
They would do it if they could
Friends that care
Stay with you
They don't ditch you for another pair
You and your friend are stuck together like glue.

Tear Jar
by Olivia Saitta

If I exposed my teardrops,
Would you collect them like a bucket of rain?
Or store them in a bucket to use them with a mop,
Or put them in jars labeled "My Pain".
Would you follow the path from where they came from?
From my eyelids down my cheeks,
As they tell the stories that explain why I was glum,
The tears will explain why I was too sad to speak.
Would you hold my face gently?
As you put the tears to a halt.
And speak to me as you coo ...
"You're too special to cry, hopefully you see
that you are worth more than the things people put you through".

To the Brave Heroes of the Civil War
by Averee Acuña

From the spring of 1860
To the spring of 1865,
So many brave young men
No longer alive.
North against South
Brothers against brothers
Brought so many tears
to their fathers and mothers.
They fought for what they believed was right
From early morning, until late at night
They marched, they fought
They were wounded and died
Hearts were broken nationwide.
Blood flowed throughout the fields and farms
Laying silent, both men and arms
The North and the South had settled their score
Thanks to the brave heroes of the Civil War.

After Hurricane
by Kayla Pawlukanis

Here I stand on land
Here I stand on the border
Here I stand on sea
Calm the sea is now
though I know when it roiled
when it destroyed all
For fate sent the storm
the roiling storm that stole
the calm sea away
Now I look at them
The land, the sea, the border
I look with scared eyes
I had been happy
Standing on the land and sea
Before hurricane
Though I feel misled
Seeing a sea so passive
After hurricane
After hurricane
I am afraid

I'm Helpless
by Samaly Reyes

I'm helpless
Can you see me?
Can you hear me?
Can you help me?
I can't see
I can't hear
I'm helpless
Pitch black and alone
aching pain down my bones
loneliness eating at my skin
trying to find a way to fit in.
Nowhere to go, nowhere to turn
Each corner darkness filled the air
Asking me to come closer if I dare
No one but the darkness cares
Can you see me?
Can you hear me?
Can you help me?
I'm helpless

We Can Change
by Trinity Tay

That boy that is called names for always being alone
Already deals with being abused at home
That girl called Barbie because of her pin straight hair
Didn't think twice before stepping off that chair
Their families watch their coffins be dropped to the ground
Six feet under but safe and sound
Tear stained cheeks on each family member
While society preaches they will always be remembered
Little do we know society is a wolf in sheep's clothing
The killer of this crime
Worthless, ugly, retard, nerd, all thrown at them, all society's terms
From every direction
Every angle
Every second
Every day
We say society is "messed up"
Yet, we never realize we are society
We can stop bullying and suicide
Instead of killing lives, we can save them
We can make a change

Pollen
by Nicholas Jaworski

Pollen in the air
Can we go on without evil
Spring go away

The Sun
by Kayla Giuffre

As the sun comes out,
I watch as it peeks through the clouds,
It makes the day brighter.
As the sun beams through the day,
It becomes hotter by the second,
It makes the concrete ground super hot.
The sun shines through the windows of everyone's home,
The bright yellow star burning hot then starts to set in the night,
the sun gets dark

Nice Shot
by Hannah Graham

My soul mate, my bro mate, pro mate
Always finding the best of me with positivity
Honesty is the best policy
She's the definition of kind, honest, loyal
All mixed together to define friend
Those down days on the sidewalk
Always end with cheer when she is here
Because she keeps my head out of the clouds and held high
The grey clouds disappear from the mid-morning sky
And the bright, beautiful, blue is released
Into the crisp, fresh autumn air
Just her joy spreads like wildfire in a forest
And she is the first one to finally cure me of my morning grump and full on slump
There has never been a day where her spirit is weak and confidence defeated
Not even a horrendous morning and evening could run her laughter to an end
Her style is award-winning
But her personality and presence is more precious than any prize
And when I fail miserably
When I fought, sought, and lost
My forever friend will merely say, "Nice shot"

Earth Day
by John Rigney

Each year we dedicate a day to celebrate Earth
To celebrate its tremendous worth
We need to keep it clean
We try to keep it green
Earth Day is celebrated from New York all the way to Perth

The Loving Cherries
by Emma Garcia

Cherry blossoms fall
And tears cascade down my face
He's gone, forever
Now I love anew
Cherries are blooming once again
They're as sweet as love
I think about him
As the soft pink petals fall
Cherries grow with love

My Father
by Austin Simmons

This goes out to the man
The man with the tattoo
The man with big brown eyes
The bravest man I know
This is for the man
The protector of my country
The man I love to the moon and back
The man with a heart of gold
My father is that man
The strong-headed man
The man who tries to longboard
Even though he can't
The man with time
Time for me
The man who loves me
No matter what I do
I hope he knows I love him
I hope he knows I care
I hope he knows he's important
This man is my father

Aunt Barbara
by Melissa Poland

Aunt Barbara
Always wanting to have a good time
Her hair was always perfectly styled no matter how she felt.
She always had the perfect outfits.
She was the first one to give me my first hair cut.
She is now my guardian angel that will forever watch over me.

Dream
by Victoria Figliuolo

One day I wish upon a star
I wish the star is not so far
I wish for hope, peace, and love
To lift up the world like a dove
In the sky you will see
Stars all around us for you and me
So just take a look and you might find
To let go and leave the past behind

I Am You As You Are Me
by Sarah Viola

Differences
Can you see them?
All we do is dress like each other
Act like each other
Talk like each other
But I don't want to do that
I want to be myself
Yet I can't
You know why?
Because this is the norm
It's what controls our lives
Like the president controls our country
If only we can change that
But no
There is no changing it
I can't, you can't
If everybody is too afraid to change what we have become
Then there is no changing this social norm
Like there is no way to escape the prison called conformity
Because I am you as you are me

Life
by Maureen Pan

Life is too short.
It needs an extension.
When the sun rises a new day has begun,
when it sets the day is almost completely over.
In a time when things aren't great don't blame nature,
It didn't do anything.
Your life is coming to an end.
Everything is on you.

My Ninja Cat
by Michael Manning

My cat is a ninja in many ways
Even in the way he plays
He can slice and dice, but also play nice
As long as you don't hide his mice
My house is his lair
He runs around it with flair
I must feed him at five
If I want to stay alive
He is always moving around
He crouches and creeps without a sound
He will go to sleep in a hat
Oh my ninja cat, my ninja cat

A Rampaging Toddler
by Sebastian Ubillus

A rushing river may be an angry toddler
That can truly be quite a bother.
As a river splashes against the rocks
A little boy screams at his pops.
A little one may be much pain
And cause his parent quite some shame.
A toddler may cry off its head
As a river smashes against its riverbed.
As a river may just flow about
A child will simply shout and pout.
And as the child doesn't turn calm
He simply just annoys his mom.
But as a child stops being angry
A river calms down to be quiet and dandy.

Water
by Grace Moore

Water is a flowing river, fearsome and strong,
As it floods the surrounding land,
Water is a glacier, firm and heavy,
As it slides down mountains and hills,
Water is falling rain, quiet and gentle,
As it hits the ground,
Water is the ocean, dangerous and mysterious,
As its rough waves crash onto the beach,
Water is a cloud, light and fluffy,
As it floats across the blue sky.

A Nighttime Thief
by Kelly Cushing

You hold a treasure deep inside you
And yet you have no clue
It loathes the fact that it must wait
It's when you fall asleep you become living bait
It creeps by every night and every time
It steals something from you, but this is no crime
We see it come and go
But what it really is we'll never know
Although when morning comes
You think nothing was done
The thief leaves no clues by the time the sun rises
For in the daytime it goes back into hiding

Butterflies
by Sabrina DiIorio

An angelic creature that catches the eye,
You see its beautiful stained glass wings as you gaze up to the sky.
People gasp at the sight,
Oh, how its colors are so breathtaking and bright!
No two patterns are ever exactly alike,
As you look at its design it is almost dreamlike.
When the light reflects on its wings its colors shine,
It reminds you of a beautiful church window that is quite fine.
Oh how they are so delicate,
But nothing on Earth is this elegant.
A stained glass, full of color and grace,
Butterflies bring a smile to your face!

Singin' In the Rain
by Jack Grube

I'm singin' in the rain
I think it sounds pretty good.
Look, look, there goes a train!
I'm singin' in the rain
When will the sun come out again?
I'm singin' under the comfort of my hood
I'm singin' in the rain
I think it sounds pretty good.

The Sound
by Alec Bergh Thies

The sound of thunder is a horde of dogs
Howling at the moon covered by fog
It echoes with the sound of a thousand barks
As it strikes down over the deserted parks
A symphony of many interesting sounds
As they gather from the many towns
Thunder is the local choir meeting of dogs
To practice singing a hymn to God about frogs
They bark their hearts out on rainy days
Asking for a midday blaze
That it creates a sound so amazing
It can be to some dazing

The Flag Must Wave
by Malachy Hennessy

We won our victory
With great pride
We went down in history
While others lost their brides
When they know nothing was here to collect
But always served their rights
And earned our greatest respect
All the other nights
All of their honor
Putting up the Old Glory
When they could be a goner
This is what made the story
Remember the flag over time,
So God will keep you fine

Obscuring Dark
by Ellie Adams

In the night, when the sun can't shine and fog obscures all things,
Once living things lay down to rest, and songbirds cease to sing,
Celestial bodies absent now, leave nothing in their place,
The world is quiet and deserted, nothing but colorless space,
To disrupt the perfect dark, heralding the day,
Comes the sun, which climbs the clouds, pushing the night away,
And once the light floods all the earth, the unseen is recognized,
And birds shall sing their morning tune, reclaiming the cold, sad sky.

Alone
by Natalie Shaker

As I amble through the darkness.
Not aware of where I'm walking.
I listen to the owls hooting.
I take one more step and ...
Crack!
I start moving as quick by as I can, not considering going back.
I stopped to catch my breath
I feel something on my shoulder?
I dash until I fell to my knees.
I cry until the world was flooded with my tears.

Terror of the Sea
by Tiffany Smith

Tsunami is a terror of the sea.
You can hear the water roaring.
People catching it on camera, risking lives
The innocent people screeching for help.
Someone you once knew was gone.
"Crash, boom," go the houses onto the ground.
A wave that can take over the town, that was once new is now gone.
Now we build, we become stronger than we were.
The storm might've ruined the town, but not us.
All that is left is us; survivors.
We are now a family.
We work as a team.
As a family
To get through it not as individuals.
Together.

Basketball
by John Marley

I play basketball
I'll make you fall
I'm getting to the money
your girl thinks I'm funny
I'm shooting all these hoops
I'm driving in the coupes
I'm balling like I'm Kobe
your girl wants to know me.

Hungry Sandy
by Brielle Hlavach

Hurricane Sandy
Destructive, wild, and vicious
All around eastern scare
Homes and lives gone forever
Threatening, murderous, and blood-curdling waves
Terror, dreadful, and fearsome
Waves rippling in a rapid motion
Crashing dead-eye into people's lives
Craving attention
Hurricane Sandy

Raindrop
by James Castaneda

from time to time
i see my days in a way
no others can see, raindrop
i am one of them, tears and drops of
water, falling and falling, only to hit the
ground, no sound, no one can hear me
my fall is silent i am small, i'm always
the one who is always first to hit the ground
in sorrow and still, grounded, dry, absorbed by
nature in which there is no soil to be nurtured
only cement.
waiting to be evaporated to fall again but during
that i get stepped on, polluted all the time
people use umbrellas and i get avoided,
till the world is gone i will still be silent.

Chicken Dinner
by Christine A. Skelly

There once was a chicken named Mabel.
Who lived in a barnyard stable.
She flew away
On Easter Day–
But still ended up on our table!

Together
by Hana Kisswani

Winter like summer
Moon like sun
We need each other as one
We work together to get something done
Friendship and love
Together we are one
My friends my family
Will always be there when needed
Time to forgive
And time to forget
It takes seconds to hurt
But years to heal

War
by Dillan Rimpel

War
instead of peace and prosperity
there will be fear and no democracy.
instead of love and family
there will be death and cruelty
instead of freedom of speech and liberty
there will be slavery
War
instead of a great nation
there will be segregation
instead of human beings
there will be killing machines
instead of inspiring dreams
there will be children's screams
War it's the end of us all
to time to stall

Now
by Patrice Kali

When I first met you, I had no idea how much you'd mean to me.
Every 11:11 wish, every fallen eyelash was for us.
I really had thought I loved you, but man was I wrong.
Now, you won't even talk to me.
Now every time I look at you, even think of you,
I can't help but shed a few tears.
I can't stand the fact that you have someone else.
I'm hoping this recovery will go fast,
but I'm thinking it will take a few years.
Slowly, sorrowfully, bitterly, despairingly, mournfully.
Now, my heart's been broken into a billion pieces
and I don't know how to fix this one.
Now, I have no more words to describe my pain.
What now?

Vogue
by Siri Vaddiparti

'Put your hair up the way Taylor puts hers'
'Do your makeup the way Selena does hers'
'And wear dresses just like the ones Meghan wears'
That's the terrifying message told to teens
Forcing them to throw on the overwhelming wads of war paint at age 10
Just like the gorgeous models on newspapers
But they don't know that they are brainwashed,
blinded by all that thick mascara and eyeliner
The don't know that the 'hot' celebs are fakes,
photoshopped from the fair skin to the fine body
But they just wanna look like a Disney princess, they wanna be Sofia the Second
Copies and clones of Carrie Underwood, seemingly perfect
But no one understands that
Belle married the Beast because she was different
Ariel sought for legs because she was different
Snow White ate a poisonous apple because
Underneath, there's a seed
That's waiting to blossom beautifully into something new
A crossover between a mermaid and a fairy, a whistle and a watch,
the Sun and the Moon
Non-conformist, different from the rest, a daisy in the middle of a plain field
Because beauty hides in amazing places,
in the deepest woods or the darkest forests
And not just on the cover of 'Vogue'

Me
by Demonya Davis

I am humorous yet shy
I wonder how the world was created
I hear waves crashing upon the sand
I see a forest full of animals and waterfalls
I want to achieve my goals
I am humorous yet shy
I pretend to be unique with superpowers
I feel alienated
I touch petals made of silk from flowers
I worry about the future
I cry about depressing endings
I am humorous yet shy
I understand others' emotions
I say greetings
I dream of fairy tales
I try to be different
I hope for what I have always wanted
I am humorous yet shy

Death
by Beatrice Zaleski

Death stood beside me since birth. I was different, sick-ridden.
"She won't live to be two," they said. They had no clue.
For I lived long past those years.
My mother and father danced with joy.
"Our only daughter would live to see old age," they cried. I did not die.
Not at five, like the doctors said.
Not at ten. Not after my first period.
I was strong; or so they thought.
At twenty two I grew no longer.
My mother and father passed into another life. One with no sorrow.
I waited for my soul to leave;
I welcomed death with open, empty arms.
It did not come; I did not die.
The doctors were wrong.
One day, death knocked upon my door.
I open it, silent and ready. I did not die.
And through the tears, I cried,
"Leave me be! Let my soul join theirs!"
Death cleared His throat. "I was wondering,
If you would like to go on a date."

Tsunami Strike
by Julia Landis

The dark mysterious water with rubble underneath
People huddle together hoping for some mercy,
while clenching down on their teeth
The people shriek and cry with tears running down their faces
As the water rises slowly, the tsunami strikes in all different places
The cuts and bruises that hurt people running for their lives
While some husbands are looking for their wives,
The houses and streetlights beg to stay strong
The violent winds sing the victims a deadly song
All of the sudden everything is quiet,
The tsunami hits and starts a huge riot
As the house starts shaking and people block off the window,
The children sit in the corner, thinking that there will be no hero
The remaining survivors are scared for their life
The town needs rebuilding as if it got stabbed by a knife
As the storm harshly comes to an end,
The victims soon learn that the ocean is not your friend

My Everything
by Chloe Reeve

I am the leaf,
Falling from the tree,
You are the wind,
Carrying me.
I am the bird,
Soaring in the sky,
You are my wings,
Taking me high.
If love had sound,
You would be its song,
You're the melody, I'm the harmony,
Pulsing the rhythm along.
I am the lonely child,
Somberly seated and still,
You are my hopeful dreams,
My ambitions I can fulfill.
With you I finally feel,
I can be me and sing,
I know that love is real,
Because you are my everything.

Spring Sundays
by William Hines

The cherry tree blooms in the sunny spring
Its little pink leaves shower all around me
In the distance the early church bells ring
It is such a serene sight that I see
The clouds are like sheep, big, fluffy, and white
The little robin flutters its fragile wings
It climbs through the air then dives, its wings tight
Nature holds many beauties, like these things
I see also the cows, eating their grass.
Peacefully they stand in the distant plain
I turn to the pond, and out jumps a bass
On, still I walk on the tulip-lined lane.
"Life is too busy," some people may say
But not when I walk to church on Sunday.

What Lies Beneath, Beauty Is Skin Deep
by Sylvia Bojkovic

A world full of people
people who used to have an individual meaning in this world
now invisible, absolutely despicable
now they all have the same exact standard and meaning
any other way is unacceptable, for all I knew I thought you were unexceptional
Sometimes I feel like the world has already pulled me 6 feet under ...
way too early ... not according to the dehumanizers, womanizers, and criticizers
all I see are these plagiarizers copying
off of each other like their life needs that breathalyzer
that breathalyzer is being perfect, one whiff and it feels better
gasping for air but for all they know it's too late because
they did not reach the common expectation, is there some kind of separation
everyone who you say is your friend or who you say
you want to be like is pulling you under, throwing you under the bus
you'll never be that person 'cause all you have is you
No, no, no, that isn't good enough
You aren't good enough but guess what, you are, just accept it, embrace it
you are who you are, you don't need to hide while the others are getting beautified
and you, you are getting denied
when you can have someone else better by your side
But you are occupied being unsatisfied as you keep getting
simplified but that doesn't matter
they will bring you down as they define you as unjustified ... conform-ified

I Am a Jewish Child
by Izabella Bachmann

I am a Jewish child
I wonder why the Nazis are doing this
I hear the cries of my family
I see the devil is all of them
I am a Jewish child
I pretend I am free
I feel scared
I touch the hearts of all
I worry we won't survive
I cry for all the lost souls
I am a Jewish child
I understand many won't survive
I say everything will be okay
I dream this nightmare will end
I try to stay strong
I hope one day the nightmare will end
I am a Jewish child that survived

Childhood Checkers
by Chaimaa Aknouche

What ever happened to happily ever after?
When imagination was a brick wall between us and reality
When our childhood was more than a part of life
But instead, life itself
It was as if the pleasure of being one-sided,
Of seeing the world my way, was like a blindfold
The covering of the world, it seemed black and white
To me, the shade grey was colorful
I made myself a cage, not knowing I was doing so,
However, I soon found out I was the prisoner
I was a clueless bird, without any wings
The cage was in my own mind, surrounding everything
The branches of my "Neverland" took ahold of me
The future seemed to be only a dream
It was a world I was told to dislike
And I did, not knowing why
Why is it so hard to say goodbye to this fake world?
If it is only pretend, why does it feel so real?
Once you let go of the things you thought were important
You realize that everything has changed …

It Must Be Love
by Michelle Magos

Suffocating and dying in this four wall room.
Growing weak and fragile, as the pain takes over my body.
Nothing seems to be bright,
And dullness surrounds me.
I feel empty inside,
As if someone took my heart from me.
Silence is the loudest scream.
Suddenly, the silence is taken away.
One by one, and day by day, I can feel.
I can feel something, something I've never felt before.
I'm too scared to face it, so I ignored the noises tell me "it's okay,"
But it got worse.
My demons are yelling, telling me "what should you do"
Without this, I feel empty again.
One day, three autumns
Not knowing what to do or what to say.
This feeling ... It must be love.

Graduation
by Hafeeza Ghany

Two years left,
Until then my pencils and pens will just keep running,
Expanding my education,
Looking forward to my special day,
The day that brags about my accomplishment and the ones I have already made,
After that special day I will still ask myself,
Will we stay in touch?
What can we expect in the future? And,
How can we make our last two years last?
We can either make a lasting impression on our school,
Or we can make nothing of it.
When it is our time to move on from this journey of middle school,
We will continue to make the loved ones around us happy and proud.
Until then we have to concentrate on the things that matter now,
Yet again what does matter?
Education,
We should just worry about our future,
This time now decides our fate and where we will be in the next 10 years,
Next stop,
High school where we will meet our destinies.

This Is For
by Samantha Franklin

For what was not.
For a generation lost,
A song never sung,
A memory never made.
For what was.
For the ocean of tears,
The waves of screams,
The monster's cruelty.
For what is.
For the never-ending pattern,
The ever-flowing hate,
The unmolded clay of fate.
For what will need to be.
For the sweeping change,
The twisted plot,
The overdue stop.

Imagination
by Emily Dalacio

There they stand,
Invisible from the world,
Only I can see them,
Only I can feel them.
If they were to leave,
Only I would see it,
Only I would feel it.
I wish so much for them to be real,
And to be more than just a figure of my imagination.
But for now, I let them wander inside around my head,
And carve their name into my heart.
Ten years later,
I've been living on my own for awhile.
Moved into my new apartment.
Imagination has been stolen from me and my mind is dull,
Constantly being occupied with the thought of taxes, politics, and work.
The doorbell rings and I know it's time to pay the rent.
I open the door,
I gasp,
And suddenly the world starts to fill with color again.

Complicated
by Nikayla Bolden

everything is complicated
stressful, annoyed.
layers and layers of anger
feeling alone and hated
everything is complicated.
heartbroken full of hate,
so scared to be left.
open up your heart I'm here
don't be afraid to speak your mind
everything is complicated.
just know that I love and care,
open arms are everywhere.
open your eyes trust your words
let them fly free.
open your heart when you're ready
when you want love I'm here to spread it
just remember I love you no matter what
everything is complicated

A Message To a Bully
by Rose Kassam

Who are you to tell me how much I'm worth?
Who are you to make me feel timid, broken down, and insecure?
Boxing me in, silencing me.
Forced to feel embarrassed, foolish, and entrenched; I can't breathe.
Each hurtful word a bullet piercing my heart.
Too vulnerable to fight back.
All these emotions clouding my head.
All these feelings chipping away at my last nerve.
Thirsty, hungry for revenge.
A tear streams down my face.
Confusion building up inside me.
No longer knowing what to do.
Each teardrop more painful than the last.
Out of the corner of my eye I see a key.
But I'm unable to reach it and unlock the cage.
I put myself in this position by believing all those mean words and hurtful lies.
I'm stronger, braver, and different now.
You can knock me down but I'll get right up.
Years from now you will only be known as the middle school bully
but I will be confident and do extraordinary things!

I Love and Miss My Grandpa
by Brianna E. Soto

I love my grandpa oh so much,
He passed away when I was young,
I was only seven when he was gone,
How I wish he would come back.
My grandpa meant the world to me,
We would sit and play for hours,
I would sit by his side,
We would hug, kiss and cuddle.
Oh Grandpa why did you leave,
I wish you were here with me,
I was so young, just a little kid,
When God took you away from me.
I miss you dearly Grandpa,
I know you always watch over me,
I know one day, we will meet again,
For now I will keep you in my dreams.

We Are the People
by Francisco De La Cruz

You can push us past the point of no return,
We shall never truly cry,
Mistreat others and you are sure to learn,
On the ground we shall not lie.
You can take away our dignity,
Yet we will still stand tall and proud,
We shall never give up spiritually,
We are together, we are the crowd.
We are the ones who have paid the price,
We are the ones who strive for good,
We are the ones who have been acting nice,
We are the one always doing what we should.
All we have endured is just so vast,
We are the ones who await the golden gate,
We are the ones who link what's yet to come with the past,
Yet we also make a difference from a helpless state.
The ones most broken keep going strong,
We are the next generations,
We will fix what the past did wrong,
We go on correcting the mistakes of other nations.

To Fly
by Stefany Dalacio

The breeze runs through my hair,
With a touch of warmness in the air.
Though I cannot fly,
This is the closest when I try.
I close my eyes and imagine
that beautiful things can happen.
I open my wings and soar,
The sunlight is what I wore.
I climb, and climb, and climb,
And now the sky is mine.
A smile slips on my face
As I fly on the edge of space.
I am one with the moon and stars,
The planets - not too far.
And although I may not want to,
I know I must, and have to.
I open my eyes to see,
The Earth, and its people, waiting for me.

Ode To Summer
by Cate Hewson

Watching the tide rise and fall based on the placement of the moon
Thank you for being there when my head hurt from thinking
Memories flood into my head, almost as fast as the ocean tosses another wave
My eyes glow orange as I watch the sun kiss the horizon,
and I knew everything was ok
Opportunities awake, as the view of a small boat arrives
Thunder throws the sky, until it weeps of rain.
And the dry sand that once took over my hair was now wet
But rain shows a spark of option, we dance to the beat of the sea
And sing to the tune of the storm and my eyes awaken at the spot of new light
Rebirth of the new wisps of clouds trail behind the storm
Escorting it from the presence of happiness
Smiles burst from the crevices of the rocks at the edge of sight
Shots from beneath the barrier of sand
Explode upward and create an aroma of freedom
Hands clap in unison to the chant of the tide crawling up and down
Because everyone knows only the big waves reach the chairs
And the small waves attract the children
And everyone is together in summer

My Eyes
by Daenna Lawrence

I wake up and I'm on my way
Do I see the world as it is today?
Do I know what my parents go through?
Do I see mostly myself?
Am I grateful enough or trying to be cool?
But in my eyes
There's no surprise
Of people judging how I appear
But I don't really care
And with my eyes I can dream
I can even dream what I want to be
Every day I watch and learn
And with my eyes I am concerned
Every day is a wonderful sight
And over the world is a wonderful light
And that light I wish to see
But still my eyes satisfy me

The Winter Descent
by Grace O'Neill

As my frosty breath comes through my lungs
A sensation of freedom on the snowy peak overcomes me
Strong, northern gusts rattle and bang against the metal fence
But I still wish to be by the warmth of the fire below
Sliding down the smooth slopes
My eyes wander to the view of the sparkling valley
I capture the sight of the frozen, snow covered lakes
And houses with gray tendrils of smoke curling up their stone chimneys
These memories too nice to last, still keep their place in my memory
My shivering fingers shake in my gloves
And the piercing sun reflects its rays into my eyes
With the snow used as its own personal mirror
The tall, towering trees fill my surroundings in almost all directions
But they still manage to stay clear of the trail lying in front of me
Racing down the steep, white hill
Sounds of the whipping wind howling
And my hammering heartbeat fill my ears
While I wait for my skiing friends to catch up to me
The bright blue sky awaits me at the chairlift
While snowflakes with all different patterns swirl in every direction
My mind fills with thoughts of all the past times I've done this before
And tons of images float into my head

Dark Night
by Jonathan Walsh

The air breaks down the houses in pieces
The wind brings everyone in tears
They see the light from the sky
Their faces are still full of fear
Everything they owned is dragged away and gone
When you look around all you see is the tearing faces of adults and children
Homes dragged away in the windy tornadoes
There are no bodies on the ground but everyone is full of tears
Many are homeless but they will rebuild
The tornado destroyed everything in its path
I jump into the basement as the winds push against my hair
My family is in complete despair
The house may be destroyed but at least I have the cellar to protect us
We may be here for days but the deaths will always haunt me
I will only be known as the boy who survived the storm
Not Jonathan, not myself, only the boy who survived the storm
It is my job to help the rest of my family by dragging on this incredible legacy

Why Weren't You There?
by Malcolm Ouattara

When I was younger
My mother did not bother
I looked everywhere
No one was there
Why weren't you there?
But these people they took me in
As one of their kin
They looked out for me
Cared for me
They were my gang family; they fed me
On the mic, I became quite literal
Spit sick syllables without principle
I quickly rose to fame
Learned how to play the game
Why weren't you there for me when the fame came?
I became a great success
I became one of the best
But I was brought down from all the violence around me
But I will live on as an unforgotten memory
Why weren't you there?

Ballet Dancer
by Lila Oranchak

The dancer on stage causes
oohs and aahs
She impresses the audience with
her spins like tops
and leaps of a kangaroo
The ballerina is light and delicate
yet strong and powerful
The audience is in awe
of her graceful
dancing

The Stars Are My Infinite Path
by Kristina Rybak

As I lie awake on the Earth's cold dry surface
I look up at the sky to see billions of tiny lights
Suddenly I hear a voice whispering to be found
I realize something was telling me to follow
I see a light guiding me, for every step I take, and every move I make
The path is still going, it seems endless
The journey is tireless, the light attracts me
I soon realize, what was calling me,
The stars are my infinite path

The Golden Willow Tree
by Ryan Rappoport

Erect, I stand at eternal attention,
isolated I am from other trees,
my only friend at my side murmurs and gurgles constantly,
my boughs arc in all directions,
reaching upwards and outwards,
the sunlight shines on my leaves,
my roots, deep down in the ground, never see the light of day,
up top, birds chirp and fly,
Down below, worms burrow and crawl,
Wildflowers bloom all around,
all the colors of the rainbow,
bees buzz from flower to flower,
Erect, I stand at eternal attention.

I Am a Puppy
by Erica Scotto Di Santolo

I am a puppy
I'm not very lumpy
My ears are pink
I do not stink
I smell like flowers
With a lot of powers
My fur is light brown
I never frown
I am a puppy

Oh Bacon
by Kyle Bagehorn

Oh bacon you're so tasty
I like it when I bite into you
You're so sizzily
I like to munch on you when I'm hungry
I also like to lick you when I see you
Oh bacon oh bacon you're such a delight
I like to order you at breakfast and at night
Oh bacon oh bacon
You're tasty, you're even better when I bite you
Bacon you're my dream food
Oh bacon you're so good
Oh bacon oh bacon I like your smell
Thanks bacon for the delight of eating you

My Moment
by Jason Singer

It is said that a person has one moment in their life to shine.
I understand what they are saying, but I don't believe it's the case in mine.
I used to think that it was impossible to be the one who has their moment first.
Who cares anyway, being foremost in class is the worst.
My moment will be when no one can tell me that I am wrong.
My moment will be when I am singing a song.
My moment will come and everyone will hear what I have to say.
It may come when I am the star of a Broadway play.
All my moments will happen and no one can stop them from coming.
I will be proud of my moments because I gave it my all, I gave it my loving.
And now I will wait for my next moment even if it takes forever.
I will wait as long as I need, since all of my moments are a part of my life's treasure.

Happiness Is Short
by Calvin Mumma

Happiness is short
Like love not to be
Like a short sweet summer breeze
Like the forever changing color of the leaves
To know happiness
Is like walking above the trees

Summer In Saint Petersburg
by Laurel Minde

we're wheeling through all these crowded rooms
'cause the heavens said: "You're so young to be dying so soon"
but she called me a wide-eyed child with stars in my veins
fragments of Lucifer's broken heart and his lover's remains
we acted as though our orange juice was mixed with vodka shots
Canada sent its regards in packs of menthols, our rotting thoughts
and though she called me a wild-eyed child with arsenic in my veins
you can fossilize my scars, you won't take away their pain

An American Game
by Gianna I. Panzera

Courageous look in your eyes.
Your bat swings up.
Your sweaty fingers clutch the bat.
The pitcher looks you in the eyes, the ball comes racing to you.
You lift the bat and swing.
The crowd in the background stands up and starts cheering.
You look up to see the ball flying and you run,
as fast as you can like your life depended on it.
Making your way to third base.
The ball is thrown to second.
You glare with fury.
You drop and slide home.
"Safe," the ump yells.
You get up and you feel like you're on top of the world.
Everyone yells your name in cheer.
Boys invented it, girls perfected it.
This is softball.
This is my game.

Life
by Julia Knox

Could there be another universe that we may not know?
There could be planets of sunshine or all be covered in snow,
They might have brighter stars or no atmosphere.
Who's to tell us if there is more life and where?
All my life these thoughts have been somewhere in my brain.
Maybe there's more knowledge of this that humans will soon gain.
Everything could be wrong and life may be an illusion,
If so, then I guess we're just toys of its confusion.

My Friend
by Gianna Targia

A friend is one who knows you well
With secrets that they'll never tell.
They're there for you and seem to know,
What you like and where to go.
You spend some time to laugh and share,
Or play a game of truth or dare.
They will know when you feel blue,
And always be there just for you.
It's fun to share your wants and goals,
As if you're one but still two souls.

A Tower's View
by Sofia Ospino-Lopierre

I'm a tower standing tall
No kingdom I protect shall fall
So high I can see the great skies
You can trust me, it's no lie
People can climb up and down
You climb me, you're high above ground
Night, I'm a watchtower then
That's where my fun comes to end
I groan when you step on me
Look and see the forest of trees
I'm made with stone, I'm so old
I'm not wood which crawls with mold
Attackers are coming near
Now they are attacking me here
No one is able to see
The great peril coming near me

Poems and Poets
by Marcel Gomes, Jr.

It starts out with pencil and paper.
The pencil flows freely through the hands of a poet
all his thoughts written out on a piece of paper.
For all the world to see.
He expresses the feelings of his heart,
but he doubts himself now and then.
But at the end hope, faith and courage
bring him back on his feet again.
He writes about flowers, animals
and life, and all its strife.
Then finally the moment comes.
He takes a deep breath.
He puts down the pencil.
And takes a step back,
he looks at his poem with pride.
For his masterpiece is done.
And the moment was his to seize.
he knows not what others will think,
but it is beautiful in his eyes.
and that's all that matters to him.

The Love That Can't be Compared
by Nicole Ronquillo

Love, such a strong word only used for someone special
the person who lives within a heart, the soul is put in the hands
with the one who was chosen to be trusted
Once this person is met, you know your life is good in their hands forever
The chosen one, to care for me always, to hug me when needed
to understand me when I felt lonely, the one who makes me feel like
I don't need anyone else in the world but them
the one who shares their pain, their hopes and dreams
to help you make the right decisions, to not make the same mistakes
this special someone is my mom
Just because we are connected for life she will always be my hero
My savior, my everything
Just because of the type of love that is given
by words, actions, and just by feeling it inside of you
like if you have never had a soul in you
It was sucked out from you since your birth and put back
It's the feeling of the type of love
The love that can't be compared

Polaris
by Alissa Sherbatov

I am a star
Taller than man
And when I fall, I rise again.
There are stars near Leo, the Celestial Bear
There are millions and billions of me everywhere.
In my world live comets and nebulae
And white dwarves and meteorites also may.
But the black holes always get their way
Their mood is always grouchy and gray.
During the night, I am used to attention
"That star over there" is all I hear humans mention.
When the sun rises, I can't say or tell
I don't have a voice for goodbye or farewell.
I am a star
Taller than man
And when I fall, I rise again

The Love of My Life
by Marygrace E. Sicheri

Although I don't see you anymore,
You are definitely in my heart.
I'm never letting go,
My strong knight.
You are my light,
Most certainly my life.
You are strong,
Stronger than me.
Definitely an inspiration.
You served for many,
Risking your life,
You were brave,
Forever my favorite.
You know I love you,
Day in and day out.
As I kneel at your grave mourning,
I hold our son's hand.
He says, "Mommy don't be sad, I will protect just like Daddy did."
We say our prayers and say goodbye,
I love you, my soldier, my brave, brave soldier.

Friends
by Emily Bruce

Faithful
Reliable
Irreplaceable
Encouraging
Nice
Daring
Silly

Tre
by Courtney Martin

My dog is my best friend
He comforts me when I am down
He is a reason I get up in the morning
He is a light in my life
I would do anything for him
When I fall asleep at night he is there
When I wake up he is there
I love him dearly
He is close to my heart
But when I have company
We are miles apart

From Heaven
by Zoe Pace

Looking down, I feel proud
I see the world, I see it swirl
I see my family living happily
As I watch them from above, I hope they feel my special touch
For the kids I left hugs, for the family I left love
Though you might grieve, but look up and you will see me
I am watching you, from above, watching with love
From Heaven I watch, never taking my eyes off the clock
I know you want me back, but I am in the past
I am in your heart, we will never part
I want you to smile for life only lasts a while
For soon you will be with me, up above the trees
Looking from Heaven
Looking back and smiling

Ode To Oreo
by Grace DeCarlo

Beautiful white princess of creams,
Protected by her cookie knights in their bold, black armor.
The vulnerable dessert,
At risk of the enemy.
At risk of being eaten.
Its dark and white manor, crumbling at single touch.
The dunk suspends them all.
The cold, wet milk, surprisingly good, feels like a dip of the pool.
The enemy takes it by surprise,
It attacks, taking out nearly half the army.
The kingdom's at risk. The risk of crumbling.
At risk of the bite.
Oh, farewell, mighty knights and beautiful princess.
How well you fought.
How nice your kingdom was, how tasty it was.
Oh, Oreo, how delicious you are.

The Cursed and the Gone
by Caitryn Tronoski

Cursed is the bringer of devastation
Gone is his blackened soul
In comes the storm, the rain and the lightning
The thunderclouds boom, in they roll
For the twisted purpose
Means a twisted mind
Through dark actions spells will bind
The wretched impulse,
Wretched thought
To the evil that it sought
A blessed heart
And blessed soul
Before dark magic took its toll
So clearly, as it's been so long,
He's cursed and he's gone
The cursed and the gone
Have no greater part
Than to be evil,
Dead of heart
So denounce the curse from the very start.

The Auto-Biography
by Caleb Salters

Caleb
Brave, bold, loving, smart, determined, and musical
Son of Jennifer and Darryl Salters
Who loves football, basketball, cake, reading, adventures, and horror movies
Who has felt lonely, sad, happy, mad, and left out
Who fears paranormal activity
Who won the Pop Warner Football Championship
Who dreams of being a professional football player
Who is from New Jersey
Salters

The Antagonizer
by Sienna Volpe

She was in the back of my mind.
I was trying to forget her.
All of the things she's done to me, has done nothing but hurt me.
Friends but now not.
Talks about me behind my back, telling her friends how horrible I am.
She bullies me and teases me.
SHE HAS TO STOP!
I ignored her, I avoid her, I try to push her out of my mind.
Hoping that someday she will float away like a balloon rising into the sky.

Skating
by Darby Metz

The silky touch of their presence on my feet
Like wings getting ready for flight
The ice is slick and smooth
With the aroma of sweat and hard work
Fills the gaps in the air
I glide onto the ice
Forgetting my surroundings
Like flying away on frozen dreams
I imagine the soft sky
Staring back at me
The only thing to guide me
Is the twinkling stars
With the moonlight brushing across my face
I let all the thoughts out of my flowing mind
And skate

My Tote Bag
by Enzo Soltani

This is my tote bag
All tattered and torn
So ugly
And worn
This is my tote bag
It looks like it came out of a dump
It's blue
And it's a lump
This is my tote bag
I despise it, I do
But in it
You will find a surprise for you

Myself
by Bridget Perez

Bridget
Musical, dark, kind, and creative
Daughter of Mercedes and Luis Perez
Who loves ferrets, nightcore, anime, and Minecraft
Who has felt darkness, happiness, and curiosity
Who fears clowns, public speaking, and singing in front of people
Who has accomplished taking care of a ferret
Who wants to experience Vidcon and visit Tokyo, Japan
Who is from New Jersey
Perez

Dark Sunshine
by Alexa Perez

The girl hugs herself and stares at her shelf.
At the shadow of a doll being cast across her wall.
And to think that she'd get up and see a picture of her family.
The girl sung a long sad song.
She knew there was no one to sing along.
But of course the child had the gall to look back at her shadowed wall.
And she allowed herself to crack a smile; the first one after a while.
Just like that a ray of sunshine came;
So bright it would bring a summer day to shame.
The birds hummed and the flowers bloomed.
The voices of the city choir boomed.
All because of a little girl's grin, despite what happened to her twin.

What To Write?
by Isabelle Papa

Mind empty. I can't think of anything.
I've tried and tried, and my page is blank
No, I'm not going to write about spring.
I've stared for awhile now, there is nothing
All hope of writing a good poem has sank
I'll attempt to write about a new thing.
Waiting for the bell to sound with a ding
It's only my teacher that I can thank
No, I'm not going to write about spring.
Maybe a bulb in my head will go "bing"
Could I write about diving, with a tank?
I'll attempt to write about a new thing.
The birds outside are now starting to sing
I tried to write about that, but it stank
No, I'm not going to write about spring.
I'm done. It's over. I'm finished writing.
I'm sorry, teacher, my page is still blank
No, I'm not going to write about spring.
I'll attempt to write about a new thing.

Chatting
by Lilian Williams

You hear them speak ... again
This was the thousandth time
It was a conversation that had been going on for two hours
Only about themselves
They had starting repeating themselves
They liked art and baking
Rock climbing and soccer
What else is there to know
I heard the same story twice
The one about the drowning dog and she saving it
Many details changed
First it was right outside her lake house
Then it was during one of her many surfing lessons
I started to reply, then yet another story
This about her many parties I was not invited to
I start to yawn and shift my seat
She does not pick up on any of the hints
As she picks up her phone while talking to me again
I walk away telling myself my stories

Our Heroes
by Lauren Kim

Like layers of an onion
We need protection
To sleep in peace
To walk in joy
To plan the days ahead
Helplessness isn't my favorite word
Fear isn't my favorite feeling
Insecurity is my least favorite
Hopelessness isn't what God wants us to feel
This is a special day
Because we are protected
By the veterans
Who help all of us
To sleep in peace
To walk in joy
And keep the harm far far away from us

Days of Distress
by Shay Huetz

Sometimes I think
One simple word.
How?
I hear a whine,
A bark
A cry
Animals are happy beings
Bringing joy
And sucking out sorrow
Who would even have the heart
To beat them so cruelly?
Bruising and battering
Changing their souls
I see today so many pets
Cats and dogs
So shy and scared of the human race
One step and they run
One voice and they jump
We try to help
And they die

The One
by Farah Crespo Mahmood

I waited in the vague night
The twilight was a bit of a fright
Boom
I waited near the tomb
Was it lightning?
Or was it something frightening?
Was it a soul?
Or some type of three-dimensional hole?
Was it the soul of Old McBold?
Was he unpresumptuous or just without a doubt old cold?
I felt like another person
I felt my senses worsen
I finally found that I was the one
My time was done
Bye, bye, bye
I cry very, very high

I Am Taylor
by Taylor Anderson

I am happy and glamorous
I wonder how people can watch *The Walking Dead*
I hear a unicorn galloping
I see a unicorn over a magical rainbow
I want Snapchat
I am happy and glamorous
I pretend to be Ariana Grande
I feel a unicorn's mane
I touch a rainbow
I worry about my friends and family
I cry thinking about my dog dying one day
I am happy and glamorous
I understand that I'm growing up
I say that DANCE is life
I dream about running through a beautiful meadow
I try to work on my splits
I hope that in dance I will be able to learn pointe
I am happy and glamorous

From Time to Time
by Maya R. Lee

From time to time I like to gaze
up at the starry sky
and I wonder what it would have been like
if we did not abide
by society's cruel rules
and inhumane ways
of social isolation
and the stereotypical phrases
and the labels based on faces
and the judgment of color, gender, and races
and in those moments
I wonder
what would it have been like
in a world
without the common hobby
of hate

Watchful Eye
by Gwendolynn Saint-Hilaire

I see you my dear growing in beauty
I shall always love you no matter what, it is my duty
I see you worry
But remember the path of life isn't so blurry
I hope you have a fresh start
Remember to keep your pure heart
Good luck with college I am so proud
I want you to know that even if I am high above in the clouds
You will do great
You are choosing the best path, it is your fate
You are becoming such a great person
The amount I miss you will always worsen
My only regret is that I wasn't with you every day
May your days not be grey
Always remember to make the right decision
Just because I am in Heaven there will be no division
Don't you shed a tear my dear
I will always be here
I am proud to call you mine because I will always keep a watchful eye

The Time Traveler
by Sarah Chavez

Imagine what it would be like
To be able to time travel,
To see the future, and the past,
To see your firsts, to see your lasts.
What if you met a dodo bird,
Or drove in a flying car?
What if you watched dinosaurs roam,
Or toured a futuristic home!
Imagine hearing a loud "Whoosh",
Which was a drone flying pizza!
What if you heard a cannon's "Pow!"
You were in Gettysburg, but how?
This is all thanks to time travel.
Because of time travel, you can–
Hear the first telegraph,
Or see a 3-D photograph!

One Man Had a Dream
by Marko Eliyashevskiy

One man had a dream
He saw men of all races
With smiles on their faces
Together joining hands
People from different lands
People of different culture and creed
Coming together that is all we need
One man had a dream
That made us all gleam
Even in times of fear
At the end of the day we would cheer
And make it clear why we are standing here
All together hopefully forever
Knowing all of us endeavor
Saying no to bullets
Living life to the fullest
Saying no to bullying
Knowing we are ruling
Let's make this dream come true
Let's make our voices break through

From the Outside In
by Addie Cope

From the outside in,
First is your skin,
It's your armor and protective coating.
Then comes your blood,
It dries dark as mud,
And keeps you up when you're a-floating.
Underneath's your muscle,
It's what makes you hustle,
And helps you scratch your nose.
Then of course,
Just like a horse,
We all have plenty of bones.
They're what keeps us upright,
Without them we'd be a downright,
Muddle and puddle of clothes.

Memories
by Madison Camacho

Memories.
They come and they go
but, the ones that stay - mean something.
Childhood memories are the best.
All the joy and laughter,
like riding an unsteady roller coaster
of adolescents.
As growing young men
and women, we see life as
a struggle, little did we know the real struggle
is growing up.
We were careless and had little to worry about.
Now as adults, we would do anything
For playtime outside
or even chasing the ice cream man until you couldn't
catch your breath.
The struggle used to be not getting what you
Wanted or being put in timeout. And now we worry
About raising a family or "How are we going to pay for this."
Oh how we wish for our childhood back.

This
by Abby Tuorto

Well this, this love, it shall never happen
No, I cannot, cannot ever let it
Well I, I allowed myself, I fell in
When it was still early, I should have quit
In the end, oh yes, they will all break me
But they already have done– it was just, some
I am not able, I cannot be free
but they are able, and they can kill them
you know I do want, I wish to forgive
Why must I forgive? That I do not know
So I may, please, continue on and live
So I can watch the wind, let the wind blow
just know love is not, it is never true
and know that in the end, neither are you

Dulce Bellum Inexpertis
by Kristiana Kuras

The battleground is empty.
Because it is not one yet.
But somehow they all know
The troops were an inevitable threat.
The blood is yet to be spilled.
The pain yet to be endured.
But somehow they all know
That their frightened minds will never be cured.
And they will move in, they'll come!
And they're hiding in their cellars!
But somehow they all know
There will be many new, distant dwellers.
Soldiers are going to yell.
Cannons are going to roar.
And somehow they all know
Their lives will never be same anymore.
They are vicious and fighting.
Neither side is letting go.
And somehow they all know
The plentiful blood is going to flow.
Why do they make them do this?
Why do they think it is good,
When all the soldiers would see
Is Death where it stood.

Life
by Rudolph Lundy

Many things don't last but the most precious is life.
People might say money, or food, or playing a game.
Everyone knows all that is lame, people love money,
but everyone wants to live
Without life you won't know how much you can achieve.
Without life you don't know much food, games, or money you can receive.

To Some of Us
by Ines Avila-Mota

To some of us,
there is no God,
there is no hope,
and there is no hope to be any better.
Some of us are just empty.
Our minds are blank
Our eyes do not have any words.
Love is the only thing we believe in.
We stand by it,
we fight for it,
we hope,
we wish and we give up.
Because to some of us love is everything.

Invisibility
by Grace McAndrews

I'm one of 7.4 billion
I'm just another person in the crowd
People come and go
But no one ever sees me
Even if I put on a show
Who would know
Because I have a curse of invisibility
I will and have never been seen
5678 days, 149.9176 months, 651 weeks, 109439 hours, 6566398 minutes
and I'm still invisible
I can't flee
For I am me
Cursed with invisibility

The Grass
by Allie Fugate

I lie with the grass on my back
While the dog snacks on feedback
The sun keeps its distance
We are still coexisting with no path of resistance
True with one another
Just like me and my mother
As I lie on my back in the grass

The Beach
by Alex Pane

At the beach
the towering ocean waves
attacking the soft powdery sand
the scent of the sea
the view of the water
the taste of the sand
the oyster called life
all in the palm of my hand

For She Is Me
by Ava Callas

She lay awake at night in bed,
With the awful words running through her head.
She didn't know where, but she wanted to go,
For everyone now seemed to be her foe.
Without hesitating she went into the dark night,
She made sure she was nowhere in sight.
She started out walking then began to run,
For she knew the awful people were never done,
With their insults and rude torture,
They would never stop, she knew for sure.
She sat down and began to cry,
And to herself she told a lie.
She told herself she would get through,
But she knew there was nothing more she could do.
She knew the crying would never stop,
Until she cried out every last drop.
I know you're wondering who "she" could be,
But the mystery is solved, for "she" is me.

Dreams
by Margot Motyczka

When I think,
I dream.
And when I dream,
I dream about changing
the failures to successes.

Change
by Daisy Andrejco

In a well devised path, it flows forward
A sparkling consistency of same
Day after day the same piece of nature
Lacking criticism and lacking shame
But what about when the flow turns about
Or freezes over;
Disappears in a drought?
What about when the ferns are left to wilt
Or the parched deer flop over, lifeless
Does it leave us with sadness, or with guilt?
Does it leave us with pleasure or bliss?
When the flow becomes entirely anew
Will there be anything more for us to do?

Where I'm From
by Joseph Szanto

I am from king size Kit-Kats,
From my Swegway I ride around town,
And from Daft Punk.
I am from the baseball I throw,
From the bat I hit it with,
And from the friends I play with
I am from Twix and Snickers,
From Alex Ovechkin and Marty Brodeur
From "Live life to the fullest" and "Do or die"
I am from Melanin Martinez
And from the hockey I play.
I am from shooting on my net,
From JJ Watt and Alex Rodriguez.
I am from the T.V. on my wall
That plays Blue Mountain State
All night long.

Dreams
by Victoria Caliendo

Dream with your imagination.
Run wild in the wind.
Evolve around your creativity.
Admire the good things in your past.
Make use of the bad things,
Soon you will awake from your nightly sleep.

The Flowers
by Emily Huang

Once, when I was little I sat and stared,
As the flower buds grew high in the air.
They explored the sky,
As I lifted them high
And each day would grow and grow.
One day I didn't check up.
I should have known better.
I went outside, with my head a bit tilted,
And discovered they were wilted.
So I cried and cried,
With my hands covering my eyes.
So the next day, I wrote a small letter,
Promising that I would get better.

A Poem In a Poem
by Nathaniel Havens

I have nothing to write about,
I must unfortunately say.
I must have writer's block on this beautiful day
Yes, there aren't any good ideas a-flowin',
And my mind isn't enchanted or growin',
Maybe I'll write a limerick,
Yes I'll rhyme!
And have a marvelous time!
Or a haiku and have a set number of counts
Five, seven, five yes, that's the amount
Mmm, too simple, a free verse poem will do!
No, too vague, I like limits, you know it's true
Well back to square one,
And hey, look at that, I'm done.

Soccer
by Rebecca Schlutter

In soccer you run
You play out in the sun
On my hair I wear a bun
I just have so much fun

Learning To Bake
by Tara Rico

Milly wanted to bake a cake
The problem was she could not bake
Then she looked at some cookbooks
Milly wanted to bake a cake
She put all the ingredients in the oven and had to wait
Then Milly look up some cooks
Milly wanted to make a cake
When she took the cake out of the oven it looked like a cupcake
The cake was as little as a notebook
She tried it again and had to wait
The second time she baked the cake it looked great
Milly had learned to be a cook
She had learned to bake a cake

Seal
by Emma Bruce

As I watch the seal pass me
I wondered if he would
Care about what people
Say if he could understand
He zooms past me
Without a care
He swims with pride
With a swerve and a twist
Why would he be so happy
In a world like this
Where people talk about you
And say rude things
Why would a seal
Swim with pride and
Without a care

Time Moves On
by Allie Mishkin

I had a broken watch of gold,
But still young turns to old
Through the passing hours,
The buds all bloom to flowers
The chicks will leave their nest,
So the mother can finally rest
Things will come and go,
Time won't take it slow
Eternally

A Tree Alive
by Matthew Bernardino

I had a tree
It smelled like tea
Once it grew
It was so true
It had arms and legs
As thorns and horns
And the tree began to talk
Then it started to walk
Once it talked
I screamed and ran
Then I saw the tree
Then started to scream

Where I'm From
by Jake Montena

I am from the video games
from the baseball I use every spring,
and from the football I watch on Sundays.
I am from the Dude Perfect show,
from Kevin Durant and Aaron Rodgers.
I am from Hershey bars to Thomas the Train,
from rec baseball,
from David Price and David Ortiz.
I am from Daft Punk,
from "Pedro Martinez,"
from the Boston Red Sox,
to the Green Bay Packers.

Under the Sea
by Mia Kivlehan

As I open my eyes, I look upon fish,
I glare at them as if they were on a dish,
they swim in the blue ocean,
and come as if in slow motion
I start moving, but something pushes me back,
I look behind me and it is something yellow and black,
I see another diver and he points me to the reef,
we swim down and find a hollow cave with a sigh of relief,
the cave is our shelter but not for so long,
when we get out we see something big and strong,
it has many teeth and big dark eyes,
It looked very big but didn't seem very wise,
we both are nervous and scared,
because it won't do anything but glare,
we swim the other way but it doesn't follow,
we swim out of the cave that is hollow,
we go up the shore and see,
a piece of land where we can live happily.

Where the Water Was Teal
by Brianna Worrell

There was a day
I was on my way
To where water was teal
And I spotted a seal
I watched and watched
Till the end of day
To see all his tricks
And if I had to pick
My favorite trick
I would choose
Without any boos,
But with many whoos
The one when the seal
Where the water was teal
Would do his flips and twists
His ending was clear
He would make a swoosh and splash
And even sometimes a full mouth of fish

Frightened
by Aaron Van Lenten

Frightened is the word for scared
Frightened is used in many ways
It is a feeling
One that won't go away
It comes from the brain
That's what triggers it all
Sometimes when big
But most common when small

The Seasons
by Adrianna Busset

Summer brings back the nice hot sun,
While all the kids are having fun.
Kids find seashells in the sand,
And the others get a nice sun tan.
While we watch winter disappear,
We welcome summer which is drawing near.
Since winter is getting closer,
We know summer is almost over.
As we watch the white snow,
It looks like a winter wonderland show.
But always just remember,
That winter's snow begins to fall in late December.

One Day
by Nicole Amador

One day someone will walk into my life
A perfect relationship would be nice
We will have our ups and downs
And smiles and frowns
But in the end we'll be great
We'll be together till the end no matter how much hate
You will forever always be my partner
And there's no way we will ever departure
I will give you devotion and all my emotion
And we'll be the best couple in motion
For one day my special someone will walk into my life
But for now, just thinking about it is nice

Starbucks
by Gaeun Kim

Hundreds of choices getting into trouble
A caramel frappuccino
A vanilla frappuccino
I wish I had two mouths for eating double
Smell hot coffee on a tiring morning day
Then drink and taste a hot coffee
Hot coffee helps you to be free
Smell a cup of hot coffee on morning day
Taste hot chocolate on a cold snowy day
Then tastes, smell a hot chocolate
Hot chocolate smells favorite
Taste a mug of hot chocolate on cold day
Drink very hot green tea on a drowsy day
Then taste and smell a hot green tea
Hot green tea helps you be carefree
Drink a cup of green tea on a lazy day

Today I Am Going To Die
by Valeria Gonzalez-Pichardo

It is dark, completely dark
I cannot see, but I'm in agony
In pain I lay, with nothing I can say
A second flashes by and I can only hear the same words
"Someone help, please help"
Then, I hear myself yelp
Boom! A minute passes and I lose my sense of sound
I cannot hear anything
Not even the panic all around
Three seconds pass and I completely lose my sense of touch
I can't feel where I am not even my own heartbeat
I felt like I was in a hot seat.
A few seconds later, I lost my sense of taste
The air felt dryer than ever before
A split second later, I fell from wherever I was to the floor
That was it
I lost my sense of smell
A few seconds later, I couldn't breathe at all
Then, I knew way deep inside
That today I was going to die.

Dribble, Dribble Down the Court
by Myles Cabbagestalk

Basketball is my favorite sport to play.
I like to play it every day.
I like to watch it on TV
It's the sport that is for me.
I like to shoot hoops.
Watch me dribble and make big swoops.

Friendship
by Rose Bird

Friends should be honest.
Reach our goal of perfect friendship.
Isn't it nice to go the the mall with a friend.
Eating together is fun.
No one should have to be without a friend.
Deer have friends too.
Sisters should stick together.
He's not as important to her as I am.
I will always love you.
People can be mean, but friends should always be together.

The Flower That Grew
by Stacy Gomez

Life is like a flower
Time flies by the hour
Spring is here in the air
You can see it everywhere
As the rain falls
And sunlight calls
Sprouting bulbs form
And seeds transform
Life is like a flower
Now they are as big as a tower
Sometimes they fall like a delicate wall
But all are here to crawl
Flowers are the souls of the ground
As they go up they must come down
They are with us for a short time you see
They come and leave peacefully

Honor
by Fiona Griffin

Honor
your scars
and
story.
Together,
they can
illuminate
DARKNESS

Where I'm From
by Mckayla Gardner

I am from tricycles and tennis balls
And the book Kingdom Keepers
From swimming and Monopoly
I am from Adele and Rachel Platten
I am from Martin Luther King Jr. and Twix bars
From ice skating and "just believe"
I am from Almond Joys and the Seahawks
I am from the forgotten pictures
In a dusty photo album
From the waves crashing on the beach

Blue
by Giulia Patti

Blue is calm
The sky
Blueberries
Blue is jumping on a trampoline
Cold
The ocean
Blue is playing the piano
Sweet
Beautiful
Blue is lapis lazuli
Juicy
A blue jay
Blue is the tune stuck in your head
A book
Kisses from a dog
Blue is the color that I love

Imperfections
by Michelina Greene

Perfect, a definition that is hard to relate to.
Everyone tries to make detections on people's imperfections
But really they're creating infections inside the hearts of many
While the person at the corner stares and watches
While they hold up a sign with the words "Conform" blood penned on it.
Where tireless arms strive towards perfection, but they'll never open that box
Unravel the string that holds the words in place
It is locked away in a corner next to the man with that sign.
See, the word Perfect, grew out of the word Infect
And it blossomed and bloomed until it destroyed this Earth
All of the contagious lies creep up to the surface of the earth
Until everyone is contaminated with the same disease.
"No I didn't do this, didn't do that." No, no one ever tells the truth
It's buried within them, deep, deep, in the crevices of their gut
Trying to escape, but the lie won the race, the evil has found its way
Into the heads, the minds of these normal people, and now they are possessed
with the horrifying, petrifying, dehumanizing action of murder
But the gun doesn't have eyes to tell the difference between a good lie
And a good mind, all the time and rhymes, all leading up to this one second
One line, one time, one sign. Two lives are vanished in a split second
With the fire of one shot, one pull of the trigger, done
The sick minds of these people think that this is okay
The people who find more interest in a metal box,
Than their families right there, in their chair, losing their hair,
But they really don't care, because their heart is bare
They would prefer a piece of technology over the people that love them
Who are watching the clock, move from hand to hand, while they ... rot away.
The time leading up to this very day, as the hands of the clock run away
They'd rather smell the scent of a cigarette, than the smell of success
They are too worried about forcing their head to feel like
It's filled to the top with helium just because their friends are doing it
The stupid decisions that are made based on
Whether or not a group of losers will accept you!
While the strand of trust of the ones you love, is becoming thinner and thinner
until you've passed the finish line and you have ran away.
There's not a song on the radio that doesn't teach to hate,
To not care about the future, to make stupid decisions based on the moment
What moment? Before you know it, there won't be any more moments
Because the beeping of the machine will buzz into the hearts of the ones who
love you. You brought yourself six feet under. Why? Because your friends did it!
A phrase that is not overplayed. Overrated, over dated.
I want to tell the people of this Earth that want to burn,
All the good that is left in it, with the fire in their hearts called anger.
It's definitely worth a fight, on which God you bow your head down to!
Wake up and laugh, wake up and smile, your life won't last a while
So much time is wasted on what isn't satisfying, what about what is?
Too many people are walking past the opportunities that they have
Because they are too focused on what 'they' will think
Decisions, decisions, not enough missions, make your mission great
For it may be your last one.

Journey To the Top of the World
by Macie Loustan

As I began to ascend from the earth below
I pondered on the thought of what fate for me would soon bestow
I gazed upon the Eiffel Tower and grabbed a souvenir
Yet no object could help cope my colossal fears
I drifted away as the crisp breeze ran through my locks of hair
Worried people were beginning to stare
I dipped my feet into the coral reef
And stroked my hands on the Sahara's sand
As I arose higher I took time to admire the Himalayas' snow attire
I took a rest on the Hollywood's O
Suddenly I felt the air begin to blow
It once again took me away
To the west where the sun sets at the end of the day
I scrutinized the periwinkle skies as its superb beauty filled my eyes
As I flew up the last few feet
the waters and land became strong like concrete
I landed without making a smirch and then there I perched
I looked only to see glistening lights and pure black
It baffled me at first but then it hit me with a smack
My thoughts swirled as I noticed I was on the top of the world.

Wreck
by Daniela Espada

Cruising down the street
Tapping my feet to the pleasant beat
Then in a flash
I heard a big bash
I then felt aghast
In the moment I thought of my past
Tumbling down the street
Oh my gosh I'm going to get beat
My eyes couldn't follow my head
I just wanted to lay down in my bed
The car just kept rolling over and over again
As I continued to ascend
It indeed was a very big crash
There seemed to be smoke and ash
But somehow I could still feel my feet
So I know I wasn't badly beat
I had but one wish
That this wasn't real and all but foolish

Photos
by Sara Martin

Time's forever frozen
You can look at it
Whenever
You can keep it in
Your pocket
Wallet
Album
Wherever you want
The landscapes
Art
People
Nature
FROZEN STILL
Last forever.

Along the Sandy Shore
by Ellen Gomez

The palm trees dance in the air,
Across the sandy shore I witness a fair.
The board I stand on moves underneath my feet
As I marvel at the warped wooden seat.
Along the shoreline seashells are scattered
The seaweed that lay upon my feet is tattered.
Seagulls squawk reverberating through the sky
Picking up the hermit crab he becomes quiet shy.
Drift wood laying side by side looks like tile
The lifeguard glance my way with a smile.
Dunes piled high, as tall as mountains
Grass sprouting on top looks like a fountain.
Gazing through my goggles creatures crawl on the ocean floor
While back on the beach small condos line the shore.
Lookout for the fishermen whose line is out far
And instead enjoy his tasty catch served at the tiki bar.
At dusk stars awake when the sun goes down
Right here in my beloved beachball town.

A Flower's Time
by Stephanie Vieitez

A bud grown from the sun,
Our life has just begun.
A flower we shall grow,
A person we shall know.
We go from very small,
To grow to be very tall.
Our colors to be bright,
Will grow both day and night.
Two flowers grown together,
Our life is to be better.
We start to shrivel up,
Our time on Earth is up.

Where I'm From
by Laci Thompson

I'm from tricycles, scooters,
from stuffed animals to Barbies and WII.
I am from soccer, cheer,
from dance to basketball and gymnastics.
I am from hanging out with friends, taking hikes,
from camping to fishing with my dad and going on trips.
I am from Justin Bieber, Twenty One Pilots,
from One Direction to Five Seconds of Summer and Fetty Wap.
I am from Michael Clifford, Luke Hemmings,
from Ashton Irwin to Shane Dawson and Calum Hood.
I am from Kit Kats, Reese's, from Milky Ways
to Crunch bars and jelly beans.
I am from *Barney*, *Teletubbies*, from *Victorious*
to *iCarly* and *SpongeBob*.
I am from *Backlash*, *Dork Diaries*,
from *The Hunger Games*
to *Catching Fire* and *Mockingjay*.
I am from never give up,
follow your dreams,
from never tell a lie
to keep practicing and always have fun.
I am from doctor, cook, from actor
to vet and gymnast.

3rd Place

Kenydi Young

Black and Blue
by Kenydi Young

Peering into broken eyes,
A malignant beast stares back at me.
Smoky tendrils, verbal flames,
Emitted by this monstrosity.
Defenseless, pleading for mercy,
Yet fiery fists fly through the air.
Slamming into my fragile face;
Crimson tangling with bitter tears.
Then it spreads, like wildfire.
Inky onyx, midnight blue.
Vandalizing my mangled form,
Gruesome shades of solemn hues.
Shattered bones, and bloody scars
Once given time, eventually heal.
But broken hearts, memories–
Disturbingly daunting to steal.
Scariest of all, these nightmares exist–
In reality–not just dreams.
Lurking, disguised, they capture you;
And no one perceives the screams.

2nd Place

Shaelyn Mahoney

Invisible
by Shaelyn Mahoney

My shoes leave smudge marks of sorrow,
as I make my way to the exit.
I hide under my hood, hair falling over my anonymous face.
Shoulders hunched, knees brushing, I shuffle.
All around me kids laugh, sucking any joy from the stuffy air.
Leaving none for me. They brush against me,
And knock me down. I slump to the tiled floor,
Knees hitting with a thud. But no one hears,
Only me. I put my hands on the floor.
It's cold, but I don't mind.
I pick myself up and take the steps down,
my hands grasping the sticky railing.
Outside at last, the big yellow limo lures me in,
And I shuffle hesitantly down the aisle. I sit next to the red-headed girl,
She smiles and my lips curve upward.
Hers is brighter and filled with an energy that I want.
She stands and crawls over me to the girl who beckons her.
Who I hadn't seen.
I slump farther down the cracked vinyl, into the darkness of the seat.
I look out the dirty window, and cry,
I am invisible.

Jamie Muskopf

Jamie submitted, "She Forgets" while in the seventh grade.
This busy student plays viola in the school orchestra
in addition to performing with the color guard.
An accomplished athlete,
Jamie also participates as a Unified Partner in swimming
with the Special Olympics.
Congratulations, Jamie!

She Forgets
by Jamie Muskopf

How old are you? What grade are you in now?
She forgets. It's a bandit that steals Grandma's past.
Like a thief, it robs her of her memories.
This persistent robber is continuously looting.
This despicable eraser deletes today, yesterday, decades.
How old are you? What grade are you in now?
She forgets. Her life is perplexing, confusing, overwhelming.
Simple tasks are gargantuan obstacles.
Possessions are lost, broken, misplaced,
and occasionally found as unremembered treasure.
How old are you? What grade are you in now?
She forgets. Often she fails to recall that her parents have passed.
Frequently she forgets that she lives alone.
Some days she believes she still goes to work.
She is unaware that her questions repeat.
She does NOT forget that all this is frightening, lonesome, and sad.
How old are you? What grade are you in now?
She forgets. One day, she will fail to remember who I am.
I dread this impending loss. But we will still love each other even then.
Love is not a memory to be forgotten by the mind,
but an unforgettable sensation of the heart.

Division III

Grades
8-9

Writing Poems
by Danna Guerrero

Pen in my hand, use the ink–
Take an hour to stop and think.
Three hours using my phone–
The struggles of writing a poem.
Half an hour to grab a bite,
Take a break to adjust the light.
Maybe a nap wouldn't hurt.
The struggles of writing a poem ...
Glanced at myself a minute or two–
Stared out my window, look at that view.
Back to my paper, writer's block–
The struggles of writing a poem.
Now late at night in the dark,
With one eye opened and my page all white;
I sit in silence and start to dream.
The struggles of writing a poem ...

Break Through
by Jasmin Alicia J. Garcia

"I felt a funeral in my brain."
It's all so overwhelming.
The ache is unbearable,
That I might just start yelling.
I don't know where I am.
I'm lost in this feeling of sadness.
I'm alone, confused and helpless.
All I see is an awful darkness.
I need to find my way out of this black hole.
This seems like I've been cursed.
I've had enough of this.
I've seen me at my worst.
I'm done hiding who I am.
I should shine like never before.
It's time to smile a bit more and more and more.
Show people the woman they will come to adore.
I will walk with my head held high.
I won't let anyone mess with my pride.
It's time I find my light again,
And bury all my sorrows.
- Inspired by Emily Dickinson

Suicide Note
by Grace Miceli

Death is easy.
Living is not.
It's easier to end it, end your suffering.
It's easier to slowly make yourself feel pain rather than anything else.
It's easier to hurt yourself rather than someone else doing it for you.
I know physical pain is better than the emotional.
It's easy to just make everything else disappear forever.
It may be easy for you.
What about the people that are still living?
I know how much easier it would be for you.
I know how much you want to end all of the sadness and the pain.
I love you.
What about the people that love you?
Living is not easy when someone you love is dead.
Please don't make yourself die.
Death is easy.
Living is not.

I'm Just a Regular Teen
by Samantha Paradero

I find myself becoming what I never wanted to be
A girl that's growing too old, acting way too differently too fast
I'm interested in all these bands
I'm wearing all the relevant name brands
Less interested in my favorite books,
More worried about how I look.
I used to think all this was silly,
Loving princesses, pink, and all things frilly.
Never used to care who they were,
yet now I care about who's popular.
Thought gossiping was shallow,
but I find myself listening to who's with who now.
Asking, did I change who I used to be, ignoring my past history?
Perhaps I'm less focused on getting the grade,
but more on my own personal fame.
And I ask everyone, have I changed?
But they all say that I'm still the same.
I wonder what has happened to me,
though I think now it's just normal,
I'm just a regular teen.

The Secret Behind Secrets
by Isabella Fajardo

A secret yelled out.
But it tried not to show its identity.
After all, it held the inside of her heart.
The keeper whispered to the secret,
"Stay quiet. They want to steal you."

The Great Night
by Jazmin Rodriguez

The night
Is bright as light
The stars glow as a right
The moon glows bright in the sky
Oh night
You shine with light
With beautiful moonlight
You have a beautiful sight
Oh night
The most greatest things
Are seen in the great night
The most amazing thing is night
Oh night

In the Dust
by Daniel Trukhin

Problems with others– we all have a bunch,
But none of them hurt quite as much,
As a friend who left you in the dust,
To whom you've lost respect and trust.
Your friends make you who you are today,
And it's all fun, and games, and play,
Until your dear, beloved peer,
Decides to slowly disappear.
It happens when you need them most,
It happens when you need them close.
But sadly, they're no longer there,
And sadly, they no longer care.
But still! Forget it and forgive!
You both have your own lives to live.
But they'll remember you ... They must.
When they will be left in the dust.

War
by Kyle Contessa

As the tanks rolled by
The bombs fell from the sky
I realized that all my comrades have died.
Feeling the wet tears rolling down from my eyes
We fought for our country's pride,
As I looked up at the sky and saw the planes fly by,
I knew it was my time to say goodbye

The Elephant Behind the Thin Tree
by Ambar Gutierrez

This emptiness inside, it's slowly killing me.
Every day I see your smile but I can't find you.
You're like a hidden elephant behind a thin tree.
You're so far but so close.
What is it about you that got me stuck in time?
Trying to find out more about you but you're too far.
What do you hold inside that sparks my curiosity?
I need you, I see you, I feel you,
But I can't find you ...

Betrayal
by Giovanno Widjaja

The worst thing about betrayal is that it never comes from an enemy.
I thought that I could trust you so much you'd never hurt me.
That must mean that I was wrong
You think that you can rebuild what was lost with a song?
Well, lemme tell you one thing,
I used to stay up all night so I could hear the phone ring.
Now all I hear is a gun sound,
One shot then you are on the ground.
It hurts to know our so-called friendship would turn out to be such a lie.
Can't you see the tsunami of tears I had to cry?
Why did you have to hurt a bond that was there so long?
Now all, all I see of you is only what dreams bring along,
A happy memory that brings,
Followed by a nightmare that stings,
Then I wake up and all those thoughts just seem to drown.
'Cause in some ways, I'm like the sun, I always find my way around.

Be You
by David Lopez

Don't feel bad of you
Doesn't matter of who you are
You are you whenever

Hockey Concussion
by Nicholas Bernazzoli

Whistle blows.
The center wins the faceoff.
Back to the left defenseman.
Up to the right wing.
He skates hard.
Gets to the blue line.
Dumps it in.
BOOM!
The boards rumble it was a late hit by the other defenseman.
The player's friend attacks the defenseman.
They're in a fight.
But he is still down.
The trainer comes over and helps him up.
He will get his revenge.

Nature's Guardian
by Daniel Reger

The jaguar kept himself low,
when he peered up high.
He moved very slow,
once he stared at the sky.
He glanced down below,
at a flower wilted and dry.
In a desolate meadow,
Why must all things die?
His chest was not hollow,
For his heart would cry.
And create the flow,
Of tears from his eyes.
His tears would then blow,
On the spirit of wind,
And with his sorrow.
New life would begin.

Who I Am
by Jeremiah Morales

I am caring and respectful.
I wonder how people feel.
I hear my family being happy.
I see that I'm happy with my family.
I want to be a great father one day.
I am caring and respectful.
I pretend that I'm a superhero.
I feel like playing video games and spending time with my family.
I touch my friend so I can help/cheer him up.
I worry about my family being sad.
I cry when my family passes away.
I am caring and respectful.
I understand my family well.
I say that I can become a wrestler.
I dream of becoming a great father one day.
I try to get good grades in school.
I hope to pass 8th grade.
I am caring and respectful.

The Truth
by Bryan Cleary

A veil of lies shields her from the truth
Full of ambition, hopes, and dreams she deems her future to be bright
She sees the world as a forgiving place, bursting at the seams with opportunity
And she sleeps peacefully, without a worry in her head at night.
She's seven years older, she's in sixth grade now
And sees the older kids aren't as optimistic as she
Confused, she can't find logic to why they would be dreamless
But what she doesn't know is that it is her who is ignorant to reality
She continues to grow, middle school is in the past
And her thoughts of her bright future seemed to be dim
She is left with few goals, which she believes she can probably not reach
But what she doesn't know is her chance of success later on is definitely slim
It's ten years later and she has a degree
Every day is a nuisance, and the minutes feel like hours
She cries in the corner, in her ball of regret
It seems like a life of happiness is what time can devour
It's near the end of her being and she sits rocking in her chair
A small tear runs down her cheek, and soon a few more
She would've never guessed as a child that she would be in this position
But knowing the truth is what destroyed her at the core

Dreams
by Cassarah Papa

Dreams are a place of desire!
Realms where you are a being of power!
Eager for prosperity in a world of sleep!
Ambitions become true!
More and more is possible!
Sleep makes dreams possible!

A Ride With You
by Zitlali Marcial

You and me right by each other's side
just like a roller coaster ride
no matter what they say
they're not the ones to stay
You and me will last forever
'cause we fit right together
we have a very strong bond
let's keep it until we're gone

As Life Goes By
by Sarahelena Marrapodi

As a child there are things you don't understand
But faith pulls you through
And your heart is so big, if it needed a hole it would take long to dig
And all that love is never directed towards you
As a teen you learn that there were lies
Growing up you believed
In so many things that were not true,
and it hurts because now the person you don't trust the most, turns out to be you
And you feel like you will never be relieved
As an adult you seem to know it all
But wish that you could turn back the time
To the days where money and power
Were never your top choice,
isn't funny how you don't care about your adult voice
And life just seems to be a bunch of crime
As you're lying on that bed
Where your last breaths you will take
You'll remember all the moments
Where your heart was pure, and money wasn't the biggest allure
And you're glad that you didn't live your life as a fake

Snow
by Anthony Ionta

Snow, oh wonderful snow!
How you glisten and you glow
Whether you come at day or night
Your snowfall is always a wonderful sight
Piles upon piles that grow
Into miles upon miles of snow
Snow, oh wonderful snow!
More beautiful than a rainbow
You bring momentary joy
To each and every girl and boy
Their fun is clear from head to toe
Now, no one will feel any woe
Snow, oh wonderful snow!
As stunning as an original Van Gogh
In winter, when you come along
I will want to sing a song
"Snowfall is always a jewel
Because it means we have no school!"

Imagine
by Sara Tobon

Why did I think that love was
a beautiful thing growing up,
when I never really knew what it was
or how it worked?
I always dreamed of
the endless "I love yous",
the lazy Sunday mornings,
the play fights that resulted in cuddles and kisses
I always dreamed of being loved,
and I believe that I have
been loved before;
it doesn't last, it never lasts
They say that if you're going to fall in love,
you might as well give it your all.
But what they don't warn you about,
after you give them your all, you never get it back.
You become empty, numb;
and there's nothing worse
than being alone at 3 a.m. with swollen eyes
and a head full of thoughts.

A Poem About Love
by Elizabeth Villanueva

I ask myself, "What is love?"
Is it something that comes from the sky above?
Or something snuggly like a winter's glove?
Then, I shout, "It's none of those things!"
Then, I ask, "Is it something I need to sing?"
Or something important I need to bring?
Like trees need leaves and birds need wings?
Not the answer, I say, "Don't be a fool!"
Is it something that makes everyone cool?
r something you find inside of a pool?
Or can be found using a special type of tool?
Then, the answer pops in my head.
It all comes together like cheese goes with bread.
The answer is just so easy to see.
Love can be found in a place that makes up me.
Love is something that we can all start.
When you ask what is love, just say, it's something from the heart.

Perseverance
by Victoria Cucchia

She was the girl that never tried.
She was the girl that never strived.
She was the girl that came home fried,
But one day it completely changed her life.
She was put in a class of eight.
She thought it was fun for a while.
But what she soon discovered,
Was that she was being treated like a baby.
She was treated like a baby because she never did her work.
She didn't want to.
She knew that she had to change.
She was tired of small books,
She was tired of not being independent.
She was ready to change.
She read more,
She talked more,
She studied more,
She interacted more.
It made her feel great.
It was her time to shine.
Her time was now.

Colors
by Kameelah Harper

The shades of green can be seen in these beautiful places.
The rubble can be found in many empty spaces.
The habitat of many is depleting.
The towers stand in their wake.
They fill the earth with breathable air.
We tear them down as if we don't care.
It supplies us with its wholesome produce.
We make it reduce by our crucial acts.
The beautiful shades of green become grey and black.
The towers that we don't lack stand in their wake.

I Still Remember You
by Sarah Sookram

I still remember the way you smell
Like the sweetest of flowers
I still remember the way you walk
In such a graceful, delicate manner
The way you spoke
Such a heavenly sound
How you looked
Like an angel from Heaven itself
And our last conversation
Sorrowful, yet full of happiness
Now you're gone and so are your ashes
As you left my tear-stained lashes

Fairy Tale
by Michelle Nguyen

I want to be a princess,
Like the ones in the story books.
I want a fairy godmother like Cinderella.
I want people to trust with my life like Snow White and the seven dwarves.
I want to see the world like Jasmine.
I want to have an adventure like Rapunzel.
I want to be thoughtful like Aurora.
I want to be brave like Merida.
I want to follow my dreams like Tiana.
I want to see the good in people like Belle.
I want to be hopeful like Ariel.
I want a happy ending in my story too, just like a princess in the story books.

Who
by Mariam Nasief

Who is that person?
Who is that girl?
Who is that creature with the light brown curls?
What does she want?
What is her aim?
Does she want money or power? Fortune or fame?
Does she make her own rules? Or live by the book?
As I looked into the mirror,
My whole body shook.
That girl wasn't a stranger,
But my very own reflection.
There was only one issue,
It was far from perfection.
As I stared at the mirror, which was now broken glass,
I realized that not even my reflection could last.

Love
by Noah Sabatelli

It feels great to be loved.
Love makes one happy,
One emotional,
One anxious.
But love has to be given,
Be cherished,
Be embraced,
Not broken or lost.
One must not question the one that trusts you,
That would protect you,
That would never harm you,
Or betray you.
This being of the Lord would never think to cross you.
Would you think to cross them?
I think not.
This being loves you for you.
These beings aren't just any other living thing;
They are your companion
And your best friend.
To be loved is one thing,
But to be loved by a dog is something else.

Myself
by Hamza Salam

We are told the lines are blurred
We know one thing is clear, we are not to be heard
We are told to stand there with no real meaning
We know that we are not supposed to be intervening
They say we can't be strong
I say that is so wrong
They say do not be loud
I say I should be proud
I will not fall for the trap
They say I might snap
I will not feel hazy
They say I must be crazy
Don't hide behind the masks
Because I have to do some tasks
Don't fall on one knee
Because I will just be me

The Sorrow of a Soldier
by Nicholas Mollica

Why does it have to be this way.
I pray but it stays the same.
I want to go back to my family.
I just want to feel free.
I thought killing was wrong.
But here it's like the chorus of a song.
They try to make us think this is right.
Oh Jesus Christ, please show them the light.
I still remember the look in my child's eyes.
It made me die inside.
He cried "Father please don't go."
The horror that would ensue, he didn't even know.
The battlefield has done bad things.
Sounds of silence for forever ring.
Hatred is all that's here.
No good times only fear.
Now I lie here with a bullet in my chest
It seems that it's time to finally rest
Goodbye my son and my wife
Despite all of this horror, I still believe in the beauty of life.

Originality
by Lidia Navarrete

I am one of a kind
I am eccentric
My opportunities are endless
I am myself
I am inimitable
I am my own person
The one thing in life I can control
I am an original

Catching Feelings
by Sheshanki Rodrigo

She had been glancing at him, every so often, wondering if he noticed.
She felt silly and looked away for a while,
Remembering what someone once told her about love,
and the dreamy feelings and that led to it.
She couldn't recall what they had told her,
and decided that it wouldn't have made a difference.
She looked up from her memories, and saw the boy's eyes on her.
He looked away, so she looked away, wondering if it had meant anything.
She went home thinking about him, his voice, his laugh, his smile,
She hadn't really talked to him, she was just within his presence,
But after seven hours of just being near him
she was hooked onto every little thing about him.
She often forgot about how young she was,
and that she had a whole life ahead of her.
And she dreamed of the future she could have,
if the mysterious glances between them ever evolved into something else.
She felt stupid for thinking that something could develop
from simple gestures such as those.
And after another encounter, and indiscernible actions,
she assumed that it had been nothing.
But she had gotten her hopes up,
and now she felt like her heart was broken into many pieces.
It felt useless to feel upset, she hadn't really known the boy.
She couldn't stop feeling down,
the same way she couldn't stop herself from catching feelings.
As she thought about it all,
she finally remembered what that person had told her about love.
"Be careful with love, don't overthink it, you're so young
and have so many chances," they said.
"Be sure not to lose yourself for one out of many."

Dance
by Karielys Gonzalez

Dance is so special to me
It makes me happy and glee
I've been doing it since I was a little girl
It's so beautiful just like a necklace of pearls
Listening to music, hitting every beat
While the teacher says to you, "Always point your feet!"
All the different shoes, styles, and clothes
Meanwhile wearing pretty little bows
Your hair has to be up in a slick tight bun
It is pretty hard but also very fun
Balance your turn and land light as a feather
When it's time to dance we come all together
Background information ballet did not come from France
But if dance is to show love, then I love to show dance

Chocolate
by Abraham Flores

Chocolate is sweet
It's my preferred food to eat.
While it's not as juicy as meat,
It's a delicious treat.
It's enjoyable when it's hot,
It's enjoyable when it's cold,
And the best part is,
It'll never grow mold!
Put it in a brownie,
Put it in a cake,
You know it'll always taste amazing
When you wish to bake!
But sometimes I dream,
About chocolate ice cream.
And sometimes it seems
That it lets out some steam.
Do you know what I mean?
Hershey's, Snickers,
And Kit Kats galore,
I know I could eat
100 pieces more!

My First Time
by Bryan Calderon

With you, it was love at first
After just one glance, I saw your eyes
My mind was filled with delight
Why I love you is no surprise
I close my eyes and begin to dream
I think about you every night and day
Your lovely face is all my eyes seen
When you smile at me in a magical way
I never saw so sweet of a face
I raised my eyes and you were there
My heart has left its dwelling place
Of all that's beautiful and rare
I love you so much, more than you can ever know
In your love sweetheart, my heart will always glow.

The Encounter
by Briana Perez

I've been wandering around, lost and alone, for the past few years.
I walked night and day and when I got tired, I would rest in an alleyway.
My life was a battleground; all of my tears, they went down with everything I had.
Days after, I found an abandoned apartment building.
Microscopic dust particles linger in my nose.
I lie on the floor of the barren house.
Not a sound could be heard - not even that of a mouse.
This has been my house for the past few years.
It gives my heart warmth and masquerades my fears.
Upon this house, goes an echo of cynical laughter.
A transparent female spirit suddenly arose; she was a beautiful, young maiden.
Too bad she was nothing but a spoiled, deceased brat.
Every time I saw her my vision just became a blur.
Based on the little that I could see, I felt like I had recognized her from somewhere.
Did she clean my sheets back when I had a home?
Then I saw her gorgeous face; it was my mother.
The one who nurtured me for years and helped me face my fears.
She was always by my side, even when I acted like a misfit.
Remembering all the times that I was extremely rude to her
and all the pain I caused for her.
She never left my side and she was always there even in spirit form.

Childish
by Selina Crawford

Children fighting–
Taking things that aren't your own,
How immature.
Men punching–
For a good reason, just forgotten,
It was important.
Petty arguments ...
Government destruction–
They killed one of my men, I kill five of theirs,
Inhumane statistics.
Millions dead–
But, only 20 years later, World War II
All death, no solution.
We're lucky if there's anyone left ...
Children with big kids' toys–
Taking lives that aren't your own,
How immature.

What Life Can Really Be
by Michael Gutierrez

Born and living like this forever
Burdened with a curse, however
Through his guidance I can see
What life can really be.
I can hear the birds tweet
And firm shaking of newspaper sheets.
I can smell perfume through the air
And cotton candy from the fair.
I can feel the touch of this bench
And my son's toy wrench.
I can sense his emotion
To his very devotion
Since that very day, he knew
That caring for me is what he'll do.
My son is a God-given gift indeed
And I hope he will remember for his deed
If you haven't noticed, I am a man with no sight
And it can be such a blight
But I'd like a favor, a blind man's plea
If you can take care of my son for me.

Achillea Millefolium
by Drusilla Zheng

At first violence leads to good and gold,
But after years it becomes frail and old,
First violence leads to a garden of flowers,
But the fruit they bear soon becomes sour.
The temporary garden is planted upon grief,
But even from the start it provides no relief,
Flowering briefly for one fleeting golden day,
None of the good built on violence can stay.
By choosing peace one chooses morality,
Chooses life, love, and good has longevity,
A path without evil may be full of sufferance,
But in the end it can make all the difference.
Two paths diverged.
One is paved by violence.
The other is justice.
Which one will you choose?
*Achillea Millefolia– Perennials that are considered by many
to be aggressive weeds

The Day After the War
by Sabih Ali

The bright colors of the American flag roared through the skies
Bright fireworks flashed through the skies, setting the citizens' spirits to the fullest
The Star-Spangled Banner encircled the small town with jubilation
The townsfolk rejoiced through the triumphant night
The night was fulfilled with "Hoorahs" and "We did it,"
Little children exalted through the streets holding the bright American flag
Soon night broke into dawn,
And there was complete silence, nothing could be heard through the daylight
Jubilation turned into depression and "Hoorahs" turned into a complete blackout
In the fields, there lay corpses covered in blood-red fruit punch
There were name tags of soldiers all around the pandemonium that had ended
Families and friends mourned the loss of their loved ones
Screeches and painful groans from the wounded could still be heard in the warzone,
Nurses and participants rushed for the wounded warriors
You could still smell the fresh coat of blood
Hallucinations haunted the soldiers, as if they were still at war
The town looked as if Godzilla had made a little joyride over the town
A human eye couldn't see one standing structure in a mile radius
Family pictures and belongings concealed the town
Once a chirpy town, was now a sullen and a forsaken warzone.

First Love
by Melany Norona

You were the first one to hold me close
Ever since we have been inseparable
Your love is like a medication dose
You and me through the unbearable
I just want to make sure
That you won't leave me broken inside
Because you might actually be the cure
To all the poison in my life
You are the best thing I can call mine
I know that our connection will never die
Because you are mine till the end of time
I know you aren't going to be my newest trend
But my heart in human form
I hope you never leave
If you do it might just be the end of me

Unpredictable
by Delaney Nordstrom

It's a hug and a smile on one day,
And a slap in the face the next.
It is the happiest to see you in the morning,
And loathes your existence at lunch.
It will tell you to accept your flaws because they are beautiful,
Then later criticize you for everything you hate about yourself.
It will share its innermost thoughts and deepest fears,
Then become completely closed off and emotionless.
It will laugh with you at a joke on Tuesday,
But laugh at you on Wednesday
It's you working over issues it has with you,
And them doing nothing to fix their own.
It's you breaking your back to earn their forgiveness,
When in return your anger receives the cold shoulder.
It will be you to make sure they are happy and their feelings aren't hurt,
While yours sit on a back burner.
It's never knowing where you stand with them
as you sort through their emotional turmoil,
But told you are "being annoying" when you ask.
It is unpredictable but I'm always expected,
To predict the version it will be today.

Summary
by Theresa Martini

As the sun shines bright
Flowers bloom across the field
With warm wind blowing
As the sun shines bright
We sail over the blue waves
Fish swim through water
As the sun shines bright
Summertime stars glow brightly
Along with fireworks

Proud To Be Me
by Sofia O'Bryant

I may be a bit crazy,
Or hyper,
I may be obsessed.
You can say I'm unqualified
I am who you see
You can say what you want
I'll shout it out loud
You won't crush my pride
Because I'm proud of what I see
I'm proud to be me
And as long as I know that
I'll always be proud of me

Humanity
by Edmillie Binet

I wake up every day wishing I was somewhere else
Where people are happier, cleaner, and I can be by myself
Everyone walking with weight on their shoulders
Not knowing beauty is in the eye of the beholder
Now-a-days money runs everything
One wrong move and it becomes nothing
Our loved ones get pushed aside
They watch us grow and leave them behind
There're so many problems we all face
But it's kind of hard finding that happy place
I take a deep breath and look around
And realize my whole world is upside down

One Nation
by Manuel Diaz

One nation,
full of determination,
will conquer and rise above expectations,
No need for an explanation,
This nation would be seen with admiration,
Without this type of inspiration,
Our world would go down in obviation.

Soccer
by Irin Estrada

The beautiful game,
The game that brings me so much joy.
The game that brings me happiness.
Every game is full of excitement,
Whether there's a big score line,
Or a very close game.
The amazing saves,
Crucial tackles,
Sublime passes,
Beautiful goals,
And all the emotion behind them,
Are all part of the beautiful game.

Love Out of Reach
by Denise Romero

Anywhere you go is a surprise
Meeting people you're so kind
All the haters you don't mind
The love for you is full of lies
The songs you sing are a crime
Your voice is my addiction
We won't meet as my prediction
Why can't you hear my cries
Our hearts beat the same but distant
As you fulfill your dreams
And your bright smile gleams
Even though my love for you was instant
I'll be another face in the world
But without you my universe is in a swirl.

Seasons
by Niall Hennessy

The winter is cold
The wind will be blowing hard
The snow will now fall
The summer is fun
Water is cool with a breeze
The beach is sunny
The fall is windy
The leaves are starting to fall
Spinning towards the ground

Headlines
by Angelique Perez

Newspaper headlines could fill you with grief.
They could ruin your life, and knock you off of your feet.
They show stories of people being horribly mistreated.
When equality is actually the only thing needed.
They also show death, fear, and destruction.
And many times politician's corruption.
All headlines don't have to be bad.
They could show you that the world hasn't gone mad.
There could be stories that bring you joy.
Like a story of the birth of a girl or a boy.
Without these things we'd be filled with despair.
And that's why we need some happiness here and there.

Brave Enough
by Jeanne D'arc Koffi

Are we brave enough to try
To go after the things that we want
Even if we are afraid to fail
Do we have the courage?
Are we brave enough to fight
When all hope is lost
Can we see ourselves having faith
And standing strong
Will we give up?
Are we brave enough to love
And risk being shattered
Just to have a chance at being happy
Will we have faith?

Rain
by Brianna Cassella

It is raining now.
Drops gently fall to the ground.
They are not heavy.
The rain now comes loud,
A new sound with every drop.
The noise is steady.
The wind blows the rain.
It feels cold on my bare skin.
It is pouring now.

Football and Life
by Anthony Gagliardi

Life is a lot like the game of football
Sometimes you take a hit that makes you fall
After getting hit, you are fed up
But even though you are fed up, you gotta keep your head up
The same thing happens in life
It can be very hard at times
But you gotta understand that everything is going to be just fine
No matter what hits you
You gotta put it behind you and start new
Life is a lot like the game of football

My Loving Guardian
by Melisa Alvarez

You are the most inspirational person
Who illuminates my way throughout the years
Celebrating my wins and wiping my tears
You will be with me when times become worse.
When I admire your actions and feelings
The more I love you, respect you, and trust you
Because your words will always say something true
So the secrets we are saving are revealing.
I remember most of my days as a child
When at night I would look out for your presence
Still today you can guard my adolescence
If I think of your jokes I have always smiled.
I pray your spirit is forever alive
Because I need you with me beyond this life.

My Angel
by Stacey Cadou

Green trees surround me,
as the birds sing songs of joy.
Your face I want to see,
this I would so enjoy.
The rain has ended,
a rainbow I see.
My heart has not yet mended,
but the memories set me free.
As I sit under a shade tree,
and the birds sing songs of love.
I reminisce of you and me,
I dream of you up above.
You have your wings now,
but yours are white as a dove.
I'll always remember you, that's my word.
My grandmother, my angel, my love.

Indestructible
by Christina Callas

There was a wall that stood so high,
it was almost impossible to get through.
A girl stood among the wall,
and she wasn't sure what to do.
She was trapped on one side
with nothing left of her pride.
The wall put weight on her shoulders.
She tried to knock it down,
but she was far too frail.
The wall seemed to follow her around,
it was like she was in a jail.
She felt extremely isolated,
and felt as if the end awaited.
The wall made her feel like nothing.
However, she showed strength and courage,
worked hard and persevered.
She learned how to ignore, and soon enough the wall disappeared.
If a girl once small can defeat this wall,
there is surely hope for us all.

Humans
by Vanshika Rana

We love and hate life
Curiosity gets to us
We all are greedy
We have many desires
We hope to be the very best
Like no one ever was
We are full of flaws
But we still hope in despair
We are called humans

Somehow
by Jesus Delgado

The world for now, seems at rest.
For all events happening, are the best.
The sun is out, and the birds are singing.
The streets are filled, with children playing.
But yet somehow, it begins to feel,
like all this happiness, isn't real.
Like all that we want, is all that we see.
And that we won't let reality, be as it be.
You only see the good, in happenings to you.
But yet somehow, somewhere, reality is slipping through.

My Loving Mother
by Leslie Rabay

You're always there to brighten the way,
Sometimes I feel like running away,
You tell me to be strong,
So I know we belong,
At times it was rough,
It made us more tough,
So let's forget about it,
Because you are so lit,
Thank you for being there since birth,
And bringing me to the Earth,
Loving you because you're my mother,
We will always be together,
Knowing you're the bomb,
I love you, Mom.

Sunshine
by Jianna De La Rosa

Sunshine the very thing that warms my soul
it fills me with positivism and that determination
that spirit and childish wonder that sense of a new beginning
that sense of adventure and I wonder
does all of the human race think as I do of the sun
does it not bring you back to those carefree days where the world was but a myth
this is what sunshine brings us joy and wonder

School
by Hannah Levy

They lock you in and there is no way out
And there is a bell that tells you when to eat;
It is pleasant for some without a doubt,
The guards are fun and sweet,
But once you step inside those doors
It is the opposite of a treat;
There is work to be done that feels like war
And the bathrooms smell like feet;
Everyone there has a different story
Where they came from and who is to blame
Some say their parents and some say the judge
But to me the destination is the same.

Dreams
by Connor Kopko

Drift into blissful sleep, imagination will come alive.
Swirls of color, shifting shapes. At night, dreams thrive.
The farther into the blackness we travel, the visions become more vivid.
Sun-streaked sky or prancing horses, at night, dreams thrive.
Deeper into sleep we travel, wonderful pictures we will see.
Soon they will all disappear, but at night, dreams thrive.
As our minds push forward, these next dreams, may we never forget.
The future, we will always grasp, and in our dreams, it thrives.
When we waken from our slumber, our memory of night slips away.
New dreams come forward during the day, our aspirations thrive.
Let us never forget our longings, our visions of how the future may be.
Our daily goals may be achieved, but, forever, our dreams will thrive.

Holocaust
by Jordan Anderson

Deportation
Removal, horror
Terrifying, confusing, torturing
Pain, relief
Freeing, retrieving, saving
Liberation

The Delusion
by Kaylah Nicholson

I'm full of confusion and I've had enough
It's time to determine if I'm really all that tough
And so I've come to a conclusion
That I'll partake in a fusion
Where I'll create a big guise
And hide under a disguise
In the end it became hazy like I was in a daze
But then I broke out and it was as clear as day
That the truth was the truth and that was that
I couldn't change it and I had to admit
I wasn't a sleuth, nor a youth
But still I remained me

The Truths of Life
by Jorge Vega

Life is an adventure full of experiences
That are positive, but negative too
And there lies the many truths of life
That I must dearly present to you
People may not learn from their mistakes in life
For they are too ignorant to understand
But there are others to help you
For situations can be solved hand in hand
As there are people who are arrogant,
There are people who are ruthless
But I must tell you very clearly
That these personalities are useless
So here I tell you some truths
That modern life possesses
And I very much do not hope
That the line of truths progresses

I Am a New Citizen
by Colin Monteleone

C- oming into the courtroom hoping that when I come out I will be a citizen
I- ntegrity is the key I need to move on from my old life
T- hinking to myself that in just a few short minutes I'm an official American
I- do, I do, taking an oath to be a citizen
Z- eal is what I'm storing up
E- ntering a new beginning
N- ow I am ready to take on what America has in store for me now

Bread
by Rachel Kogut

Thin, fragile slices, tiny crumbs not spared,
Mostly stale, yet too precious to be shared.
Each ration is savored, every piece saved,
All is eaten and grants us hope for another day.
Our only sources of strength are the slices of bread,
A single string that holds us, our life thread.
Hunger bores holes in our stomachs, emptiness inside,
Bread is important, it is how we stay alive.
We have seen suffering, we have seen death,
Bread has changed us, we fight to survive until our last breath.
We are skin and bones aching for one small piece,
Hurting one another and hoping this horror will cease.

The Fairy Dream
by Valentyna Simon

Pastel colors. Glistening.
Soaring gracefully, passing the moon.
A twinkle into the night, she flies.
Gentle wings. Fluttering.
Comforting children fast asleep.
A listen. In the quiet.
She hears the wishes, finds dreams.
Magical dust. Sprinkling.
Covering the world in peace.
A rising sun. In the distance.
Calls her back home, to rest.
Children's eyes. Smiling.
Awake to face the day.
A fairy dream. In the night.
Will guide their life's way.

Unity
by David Antelo

The birds are chirping
Humans are walking around
All in unity!

Treacherous Storm
by Caitlin Aristizabal

Starting like a drizzle
It's quiet but sure to grow
Transforming into pouring rain
In the storm with no escape
Winds pulling me down
I'm stronger than you see
The blinding lighting strikes me
Thunder louder than my fear
Suddenly the pressure lifts
It's over, I survived
You can't tear me down
Watching the sun come alive
Creating a brilliant rainbow
Looking around, I'm free

She Cried Until She Had an Ocean
by Elisa Lipkin

She cried until she had an ocean
Full of salty limpid tears, each with a timid shine
She yelled until she had thunder
Shaking the Earth, lightning scattered in electric white lines
She punched until she had cliffs
Hands clenched into fists, stone flying below
She kicked until she had mountains
Jagged sharp rock flirting with flurries of snow
She stomped until she had green hills
Rolling this way and that, frail stems reaching up
She whined until she had a storm
Trees moaning, leaves flying, twigs snapping with a pop
And then she looked up, what she saw left her shocked
She stopped crying and yelling, and her fingers uncurled
She stopped kicking and stomping and whining– then smiled
For that's when she realized she already had the world

Fake
by Jamie Wolfson

Yes I am pretty
Yes I am smart
But behind all this makeup lies an empty broken heart
I may be nice and caring, and always have a smile on my face
But inside I have these feelings I can't seem to embrace
Thoughts of death and harm fill my soul
And all of a sudden my thoughts become out of my control
I may still act happy or my smile may shine
But let's get back to reality and take off this mask of mine

New York City
by Kayla Zlotnick

Early in the morn, there is a haze,
Quiet streets, bright lights,
And as the day wears on so comes the craze,
Approaching in fleets, capturing the many sights,
Like the Empire State.
When night replaces day, the city is not fazed,
Loud beats, pub fights,
Those struggling to stand upright,
Letting New York choose their fate,
Welcome to the heart and soul of the USA.

Humanity
by Alice Zhang

Without violence, what are we?
Stuck in old habits,
Bounded by war
How will we ever break free from these chains?
Causing destruction ... pain ... and regret.
To what extent
Will this continue on until?
Will humanity be completely wiped out?
Or will we stop before it is too late?
For the sake of humanity
I sincerely hope the latter will prevail.
After all,
Evil is permanent.

Haunting Nightmare
by Jennifer Gonzalez

As the beautiful night grew longer,
I anxiously closed my eyes,
Surrounded by a dark and petrifying world.
Paralyzed, mysterious shadows strangled me.
In front of me, my loved ones were shedding tears,
My frail body was tainted with blood
The sadistic shadows grinned with pleasure
A blaze of fire spread,
Towards my precious relatives
Who I realized in no time, they will become ashes
As I awake, the continuous pain remains

Social Media Sniper
by Yegi Park

Who are you.
No one knows you.
You sit behind a glass wall, wishing you could be her.
Jealousy takes over you, you want to get rid of her.
Attacking behind an invisible shield, you think you're invincible.
Firing missiles across the screen, you kill.
The words you wouldn't dare spit in front of my face,
you spit it through a window.
You say you're a sniper,
but I say you're a coward.

One Majestic Torment
by Eden Egbert

This ruptured foundation ...
A slave she dwells
Flesh slaughters her inmost maculation.
In languish she dusts the seasoned vase,
Peculiar of what's to come
She weeps herself to unsung peace.
Her ribs,
They chortle no more
Her motivation is discarded
This trio has pondered upon lifeless mentality.
So witted corpse, her Father ushers his will
Embodied in the perception he'd soon ransom.

Late-Night Studies
by Gabriel Broadman

Early morning the dew sits.
The birds chirp, the clock ticks.
The sun peeks up, the insects cry.
Then in the air they swarm and fly.
Last night he had sat sad awake.
Doing homework that just couldn't wait.
He dreams of songs currently trending,
And sleeps through his alarm impending.
He looks at the clock, 8:08,
"Oh crud! I'm going to be late!"

The Time Waster
by Jocelyn Ramos

Sometimes life is short and is very difficult to understand
why young innocent people
Who aren't harmful, have to die in such a disgraceful situation
Because our beloved God chooses what's right!
Like a special someone who was very dear to me wasn't as close,
but it still hurts, she is gone
I would see her laugh and smile, but not be given the opportunity
to meet her within myself
Clashing into pieces burning in a cell of fire, half of me feels
like five feet underground in a buried chamber
Teared up in tears because now she is gone and all is given up,
no chances, no opportunities
And the time has given me no chances and it's difficult to let go,
but the fact is that time is short and I wish time could go back
and be there when she mostly needed me
She was my ride or die, that unconditional love we had is now gone!
What will my crying do? Nothing
But create more ashes in the burden cell I'm feeling, the torment
I'm living with this guilt within me
My heart murmurs and my brain says forget, but
What can I do if all I'm doing is feeling sorrow for her?
But I know it's time to let go and remember to appreciate those
who are dear to you because
You never know when life may take them away from you
regretting the many wrong decisions
That have occurred in your life, you have the chance
You have an opportunity of life
But freedom comes within whose inner peace?

Fairy Tale? Or Reality?
by Jessica Perez

It's 3am, and she's up, thinking, crying.
She has seen enough. All just terrifying.
Everyone thinks her life was perfect;
No flaws, no errors, but all beautiful things have dark silhouettes
Sure, she had everything she had;
A family, clothing, luxury, but it doesn't help a girl to be happy, but sad.
Why? Her family doesn't even care for her
"Living in the streets is what I prefer"
In her home, she just feels like she's dying
She always thought everything will get better.
Don't listen to others, they aren't her storytellers.
Her life isn't a fairy tale.
She isn't the princess waiting to be saved from the fire-breathing dragon.
She wants to be out of the living hell she's in.
She doesn't want clothing, luxury, or all those expensive little things in her life.
She just wants her freedom.

Christmas Greed
by Nicole Boado

The clock struck midnight and it was no longer Christmas Eve.
Clara was only focused on all the gifts she would receive.
But other than that, all Christmas spirit was lost.
Happiness, hope, and hugs? In her mind, those things had not crossed.
Out of nowhere, Clara heard a loud THUD!
Frightening thoughts began to flood.
Her bedroom door flung open and Clara paused.
Into her room walked Santa Claus.
He told her that Christmas was not just about receiving.
Santa was taking her on a trip and soon they'd be leaving.
Moments later, they arrived at the North Pole.
It smelt of peppermint, was colorful, and very, very cold.
Santa and Clara walked towards a large shop.
Inside were hardworking elves making toys for children and tots.
The elves had fun, laughing happily as they made all the gifts.
Clara wondered how they could be enjoying all of this.
They would not be receiving anything, just making things for others to enjoy.
But they were having fun together making all of these unique toys.
That's when Clara realized the true meaning of Christmas spirit.
It's to celebrate life and share happiness with everyone in it!

The Birds
by Alicia Powell

One by one, these little birds pass
Flapping their wings with no certainty of where they are going
and how long until the hourglass determines their demise, ending the journey.
Every flight is different, not one is the same, no matter if it's night or day.
Though it may look as though they are playing a game
I can assure you, this is not the one you want to play.
Life happens in ways we cannot understand.
Some are prepared and some are not.
For those who are not, don't fret and feel banned from life itself ...
just food for thought.
Why I am telling you this, I do not know ... perhaps I am a seeker myself
For what you may ask, I've answered long ago,
for my purpose and life's great wealth.
Time passes me by and my head is filled with knowledge.
As I lie in the grass and look into the sky, what is it that I see?
The eighty years or so of my life, including my years of college ...
and those same birds flying, one by one, right past me.

Heaven On Hell
by Sabrina Nezaj

To be, or not to be
That is an infinite question to hear and see.
To excel or fail,
To overcome and scale.
The answer is completely up to you.
There was once a man of stone
Stoic and poised as the body's bone,
His actions hidden beneath
The porcelain sheath
Contained within his subtle, veiled features.
His inconspicuosity
Spoke soundless words to me.
They whispered and wisped,
Little fables and nibs–
Bittersweet bites of chocolate truth.
They claimed the world was a bad place, with some good people in its trace.
Will you follow the hunchback, uniform majority?
Or will you extend to the valor and honor showering the pure-tongued minority
To be, or not to be? The answer shall achieve
Heaven on Hell.

Society
by Faith Gerges

If you wear good clothes, you're a show off.
If you wear normal clothes, you don't care about your appearance.
If you don't eat, you're starving yourself.
If you do eat, you're fat.
If you're proud of yourself, you're egotistical.
If you're not proud, you want attention.
If you wear makeup, you're plastic.
If you don't wear makeup, you're too prideful.
If you're a nice person, you're fake.
If you're rude, you're a miserable person.
If you're smart, you're a nerd.
If you're not super smart, you're a delinquent and nothing else.
Society wants you to be perfect
but what exactly is perfect anymore?
Don't try to please society.
Just be you.

Our Voyages
by Anthony Fosu

Here is where we are: Upon the great sea we call life.
Of course the great gray ocean has a beginning and an end, yet ultimately,
That is about as definitive as the boundaries of east and west.
The boat in which you voyage is none other than our own,
and as we gain passengers
We grow our families, and sail together
I cannot say that my own boat is the sturdiest,
and though uncertainty is our only luxury, I say
That my boat is my own, and that boat whish is the S.S. Family
Is the boat that I can say, "I am afloat."
Destiny in the rudder that controls the boat
Serendipity is her sails
Life constantly has choppy seas which rock us about
But I can stay afloat
While others may sink
I can stay afloat
While others capsize
I can stay afloat
Because the rudder is also controlled by hope
And the sails guided by discipline
Our boats put us on this voyage
And this sea gives us something to ride on

We Know It All
by Carly Rosenblatt

They think we can't feel their stares,
but they burn at the back of my mind,
why can't they realize we feel their judgment?
They think we can't hear the whispers,
but they echo in my ears,
why can't they realize we hear their cruelty?
They think we can't see them run,
but I hear the pounding footsteps,
why can't they realize we know about their disapproval?
Through all the poorly kept secrets,
of our peers,
through the judgment,
the cruelty,
the hate,
and the criticism,
what they don't realize is,
we know it all.

Block 37
by Megan Christensen

As the door to Block 37 opens,
we all became frozen.
When a man comes out, he crawls in slow motion.
Slowly towards the cauldrons we watch him,
he was creating a silent commotion.
When he reached the cauldrons full of soup,
he used his mouth to take a great scoop.
But not long after, he was shot.
Therefore, the hungry man was caught.
The gunshot was loud and frightening
which means the soldiers are not very enlightening.
We stood there in fear, quivering and shaking,
until we felt the Earth's ground almost breaking. Bombs.
Once everything was over, we cheered in delight.
They have done damage to us, they have brought some light!
But the joy didn't last long.
In this world, we do not belong.
So why do we have to play along?
This is not fair. Please Lord, hear our prayer,
we no longer want to live in despair.

I Want the Silence
by Sierra Gastelu

I want the silence but when it comes
I'm terrified of the girl I've become
Fighting a battle I can't win
Fighting for a girl I've never been;
I changed slowly but all at once
The flashbacks follow of who I once was
Now it's quiet all is done
I want her back but she's long gone

Spring
by Olivia Pincus

A wind blows through the entwined branches,
A glistening beam pierces the gloomy atmospheric veil,
The old, withered leaves crackle and crunch beneath my feet,
A twisted gnarled branch supports an aged crow's talons while
he calls into the forest deep,
A blossom, the very first of the season blooms beautifully,
revealing her ultraviolet colors for the world to see.

Where I'm From
by Joanna Shultz

I'm from trips to the library to check out books,
from the stacks of fiction novels lying on my floor,
and from surfing on the computer.
I'm from pirouettes and assembles in a classical ballet studio,
from Amalee and David Crowder.
I'm from Jolly Ranchers and popcorn,
from *The Selection* and *Harry Potter and the Order of the Phoenix*.
I'm from American Girl dolls and playing the piano,
from *Your Lie In April* and *Noragami*.
I'm from "Be true to yourself" and "Neverforget",
from playing the piano and Nintendo DS.
I'm from reading in small spaces and watching anime,
from being a teacher and Trident gum.
I'm from singing at the top of my lungs while no one else is around
and dancing and spinning around until I fall down breathless.
I'm from laughing without a care in the world
and crying tears of yearning.

Holocaust
by Lainey Burns

Horrifying experience
Escape was the only thought
Abused beyond belief
River of tears
Tightly packed spaces
Life or death
Everlasting pain
Starving for food and their lives back
Sickening to think about

Stephanie
by Stephanie Cabrera

Sings her heart out regardless of people's opinions
Tenacious grip on hopes and dreams
Excited about every day spent with loved ones
Positive in order to encourage others
Has a great interest in travel
Acts childish but with good intentions
Never wants to be disloyal
Interested in books and studying for her future
Every friend is important to her

The Sun and Moon
by Michelle Fuksbrumer

What comfort the sun gives me,
When she shines her perfect light,
It gives me a burning hope,
That no matter how dark the world is, the sun always shines bright,
No matter what happens here on Earth,
She comes every single day,
And then the moon peeks out from the sky,
And whisks her away,
The moon comes out to glow in his own way,
I always feel sadness when one has to leave,
Because they can never meet, never stay,
Never be in the same sky, as equals, together,
How sad it is to love one another,
But be separated forever.

Empty
by Angelica Diaz

There is this hole in my heart.
Along with the pit in my stomach.
Your face is a piece of art.
That causes me to ache.
You're just another heartbreak.
I'm the addict, you're the drug.
You're the wine.
That tastes so fine on my lips.
Tell me, are you mine?
I promise to keep my mouth a zip.
Let me shower you with my love.
While you just shower me.
Make me feel like I'm above.
I'm on the waves of the sea.
Come and find me.
I want you all to myself. I'm already all yours.
Just keep being yourself. I know she wants you to be hers.
But I'm the queen and I already have you.
The world is so cold. So come and make me warm.
I'm in your hold. As there is a storm.
You are my protector. Your touch sets me on fire.
The words you speak make my heart flutter.
Just like pizza I can't help to admire.
Hate when you cause me to stutter.
You have no idea the effect you have on me.
You give me so much laughter.
Along with your affection.
And just being with you gives me pleasure.
The definition of perfection.
At least to me you'll always be.
Once again I'll say, I'm the addict, you're the drug.
You're the wine. That tastes so fine on my lips.
Tell me, are you mine? I promise to keep my mouth a zip.
With you I'm always on cloud nine.
You are always looking so dang fine.
Just one look and I forget my name.
And you're the one to blame.
Please tell me this isn't just a game.

Selfie
by Jillian Pogoda

In selfies she looks happy but that's not really the case
She types in 'lol' but there's no smile on her face
Because a million emojis, they can't even fix
The tears falling down on her new iPhone 6
If it's not on a screen then they don't really care
Don't know that she's hurt, can't see that she's scared
They glance at her photos but their eyes never linger
They tap the like button with the tip of a finger
But if they looked closer then maybe they'd see
Her puffy red eyes with bags from lost sleep
She tries to ignore it but the sadness, it runs deep
And her friends' words of "comfort" are all flimsy and cheap
So get off of the phone and have a talk that's face-to-face
Because the stuff you see online is not always the case

Springtime
by Leila Alliu

After the cold hard season of winter,
The flowers opened my eyes,
To see the whole new season ahead of me,
Where the frosty season dies.
I opened my windows in front of me,
To let the newfound warmness inside,
And let the memories of frigidness leave,
While I let the happiness of springtime glide.
I looked around to the meadows,
To see the newfangled flowers grow,
And see how the bees buzz around,
Where there used to be piles of snow.
Even after the memories of springtime
Start to come to a close,
I am greeted by a new season,
That seems like the best over most.

Soccer Life
by Joel Xique

When they tell me soccer is just a game
I say it's not a game
It's life
Don't mistaken your life with soccer
Makes you stronger
Faster
I'm not saying it's important but it's apart of life
You run to survive
You kick the ball to move up or to get the danger out
You use your body to defend what is yours and your self
You score a goal to accomplish a goal in life
Soccer is apart of life

Water
by Milagros Martinez

You stand on the edge of the boat.
Debating on whether you should jump or not.
You close your eyes and take a deep breath,
legs bending and feet are sprung into the air.
It covers your body,
inch by inch,
second by second,
The water cool to the touch,
getting warmer by the minute.
You are now surrounded by it.
Your eyes open and see the most beautiful image.
Fish of all color, coral the brightest of all.
You breathe in and out and maneuver your body.
You swim deeper into the ocean.
Seeing everything up close;
all the grooves and curves,
all of the plants and hidden sea creatures.
You are amazed at the scenery, calmed by it.
You close your eyes and float.

3rd Place

Emily Kratz

Sentience
by Emily Kratz

The sweet milk of moonlight lies drizzled about the garden,
coating the trees in a misty silver filigree
As I hold the necklace in hands quickly numbing
And think of rebuilding the past. Here. Tonight.
The springhouse is empty now
The trellises are bare -
ghost roses bloom in the corners where the sun doesn't hit
What was once blithe and romantic is now bleak and forbidding
Filled with unpleasant echoes
I wander inside and rest my head against the smudged glass,
making a barrier between me and the accusatory stars
Smoky thorns crowd my mind
The lacy chain of the necklace curls around my fingers as if to strangle
The stormy verdant stone smirks frostily
And suddenly it's all I can do to remain
I untangle it from my hand and place it on the dirt floor,
where it has always belonged
It can keep its own secrets now, I think
I shut the door quietly,
so I don't disturb the memories lying in the dust like ebony feathers
And I hear the breathing of the night in my ears
as it follows me to the gate
Knowing the sentiency of black will stay with me
Always

2nd Place

Ella Kirschner

A Song of Spring and Sentimentality
by Ella Kirschner

We sit on the wire garden chairs
Talking for far too long.
We have crosshatch indents on our legs.
Our wishes drift away
Carried by gossamer messengers
That will turn to weeds.
Floral soothsayers foretell our fates.
I know that odd numbers of petals mean
He loves me.
Freshly pruned lawns
Irritate my skin.
We roll down the hills anyway.

1st Place

Yupu Cai

Calling Yupu Cai an active teenager
would be an understatement.
This member of the National English Honor Society
also participates in Student Council, Speech and Debate,
Leo's Club, Choir, and Future Problem Solvers.
She has always enjoyed writing,
almost as much as telling corny jokes,
which she thinks are a-maize-ing.
We're all ears, Yupu!

Wai-Gong
by Yupu Cai

AGE 10
The cashier stares me down, impatient, irritated, irked,
as my grandfather struggles to say a simple phrase.
Perfectly clear within his mind, yet somehow the words become
b r o k e n and s c a t t e r e d
all out of order, so warped that Ms. Phillips, my reading teacher,
would cry if she heard.
Exiting his mouth,
a knot of tangled grammar and mixed-up consonants.
AGE 15
Another cashier, another face, the same expression.
She no longer bothers looking askance at my poor Wai-Gong;
suddenly, I'm the one that she expects to speak.
When he whispers to me in Mandarin,
someone mutters, "Speak English."
AGE 20
That's how old Wai-Gong was when he sailed here from China,
Without a speck of English in his brain, about to gain a lifelong accent.
An accent that invokes dirty thoughts and glances from others:
"Well, he's not from here."
"Why can't these immigrants learn proper English?"
My grandfather, from a family where pride is paramount,
Swallows his every day.

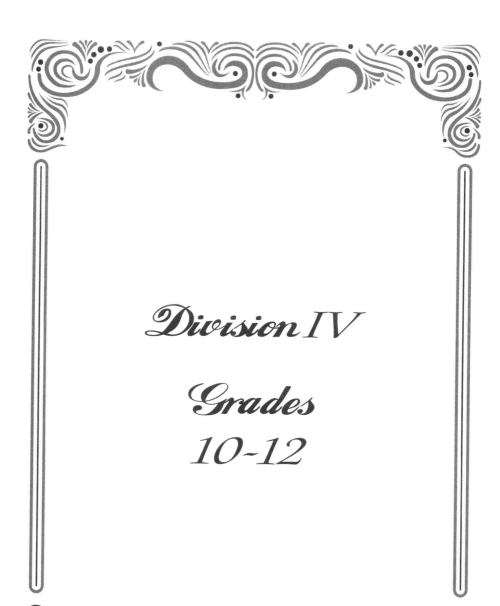

Division IV

Grades
10-12

Awestruck
by Kateri Arano

I am in awe
I wonder how he stole my heart
I hear his soft voice and beautiful laugh
I see him smile and grin and silly things
I want to know how he did it
I am in awe
I pretend that I'm calm, that he doesn't make me go crazy
I dream that someday his eyes will meet mine
I worry that someday my facade will shatter like a mirror in front of him
I laugh because I realize that I'm being silly, that my dream will forever be a dream
I am in awe
I say that he is my world, my everything
I understand that I'm just one girl, in a world of people
I try to think realistically, I really do
I question why I'm like this in the first place
I am in awe

Fear
by Chashie Komendant

A thousand minds and bodies put in one simple request: talk and get it over with,
Yet it's not that simple.
The jaws move but no sound escapes.
Mind blank, paper swimming, and legs turning to water;
Hands clamp down for purchase but receive no support in return.
Time slows to a crawl and a thousand pairs of eyes blink in unison,
My own sees but nothing registers.
Sweat at the speed of a snail,
Heart as fast as a cheetah.
Please words just come, come pouring out like a waterfall!
But no, they remain behind bars, prisoners in the cave of a musical box.
The temperature rises to that of the Sahara Desert in one second,
Before decreasing in a flash to Eskimo weather.
A single breath escapes its cavity
and a sense of calm rushes through sticks of bones,
The heart rate settles and the sweat evaporates.
While the hands still need support, the paper comes into focus and
The words flow in a tumult, the dam finally breaking.
When there's no more to pour through the gaping hole,
A resounding cheer accompanies clapping
that shakes the building to its bottom stones.
Only then do the hands still, steady and strong
Confidence breaking through the mighty storm.

Decaying
by Julia Dobel

People say "you're going to be okay" like it's a bracelet you put on
that admits you into an amusement park of cleansing.
But no roller coaster can brush the sad from your hair
or purge your anger with a shrill scream.
And quite honestly, neither can beds.
We sit in them like they're our coffins;
we say our goodbyes to the sheets and blow kisses to the ceiling.
We write our eulogies on the pillowcase.
We write in tears.
But people die in beds, in their sleep; so maybe
if we lay there long enough it will mummify us to the point
where our souls are like annoying pets we shoo away that won't stop barking.
But maybe we are mummified;
a corpse wrapped in linen;
preserved and laid to rest.
Because maybe we did ride that roller coaster,
but we didn't like the view from the top.

The End
by Eric Fuksbrumer

I can be depressed sometimes, but nobody knows.
Because I think of the day I will be buried in the ground: from head to toe.
Will my soul carry on, or will I be gone forever?
After a few years, will I even be remembered?
My friends, you do not like to think about the inevitable.
I am not sure of advice to give: philosophy or mentality.
Ironically, we will all be equal one day, black and white, the poor and the rich,
When we get buried in our ditch.
On the deathbed, we will either get sad or satisfied.
We ask, "Did I complete my story?"
"Was my life worth living, was my soul worthy?"
"Was making all this money just a huge waste?"
"Perhaps I went through life in such a haste."
Maybe I do have some advice, imagine that you will leave tomorrow,
And that will leave behind memories of happiness, family,
and maybe even some sorrow.
You would speak to relatives and maybe make amends,
You would meet up with your distant friends,
Perhaps we humans can make peace and feel all ease,
It all depends, if we can see life through a particular lens,
And see the end.

Arcane
by Ayleen Guzman

Amorphous shapeless indefinite
Repose upon formless gaps
Cursory glances at an absent silhouette
A daunted silhouette strewing upon no fiber of a being
Nebulous reveries captivated by blank spaces
Enraptured enraptured enraptured

Empty Shadows
by Yanira Reyes

Like the lonely sun shines in the morning sky
I dim down at night
Unlike the moon I am not surrounded by beautiful diamonds
I am surrounded by empty shadows– smoke
They are the residue from the burning diamonds that surrounded the moon.
They were dying but looked more graceful
than the sad empty shadows that surrounded the sun.
So what is more beautiful, the moon with beautiful stars around it
or the sun with its empty gray shadows

An Ode to Jane Doe
by Hannah Melville

Lightly dancing fingers over black and white.
Eyes closed in quite a Beethovenesque fashion.
If dancing is a sport then this must be too–
gently athletic.
She has cocaine-streaked hands like Kurt Cobain.
She's Betty Crocker with white dusting on her nose.
Her sniffling is rhythmic and beautiful: a charming addict.
She is light reflecting off a rain puddle.
She's a gray storm cloud on a sunny day.
Like Prometheus she brought us mortals fire.
And with it some hope.
She's unstuck in her life: in, out, in again,
eating a vegan breakfast of champions.
She is Gregor– thick-skinned and sweet-hearted.
They both are dying.
She has a sharp pen expressing her keen mind.
She's Parker– cynically underrated.
Razors pain her and her drugs cause her cramps.
She might as well live.

Friends
by Christian Dowdell

Pals having a fight.
Like a stretching rubber band,
each time will snap back.

Coinage
by Kyle Carlee

While basking in the stars and constellations,
A spark of vision imbues the dark matter and everything between.
This seems much like the antithesis of creation,
but breathes fresh air, and speaks louder than human words.
This magical transcendence does not only exist in our sensations,
but we also see it in creatures.
Nonetheless, time has ensued humanity to lose its inspiration,
And this destructive force has decimated
the minds of modern innovation!
Contemporary culture coins what they think is brilliant,
But neglects the absence of vocation;
Aspiring that their ideas will drift away into the iridescent
universe they call, "imagination."

Root & Iron & Bone
by Kayleigh Herrmann

Solid earth drinks from the fountain of youth.
Trees bend and break under thundering gales,
but hold on with every vestige of their being.
And then stillness, quietness.
Molten, liquefied earth. The center of all life's being, its foundation, its core.
Keep us centered, keep us grounded.
We are easily bent, but not broken.
We still stand, even under the weight of 10,000 years of grief.
We are organic beings.
We are what the earth makes us, what it wants us to be:
evolved beings capable of compassion and empathy,
with our heads and hearts pointed to the sky.
Wings take time to develop, each interwoven bone delicate like fine lace.
But mother is ready to push baby out of the nest.
It's time to flap those paper-thin wings.
Fight or flight.
There will never be an alternative.

No One Can Outrun Time
by Irene Vilgorin

A girl of five entered a race one she felt that she could ace
She ran nonstop with a reddened face
And always paid close attention to her pace
There was no challenge that she would not embrace
She ran through pain she ran through sorrow
And still looked forward to tomorrow
There was no help she wished to borrow
As she soared through air swifter than an arrow
The finish line slowly drew near
As she sped towards it faster than a tear
But the winner stood proud and clear
Time was his name, he had no fear
Tired and hungry from her difficult race
The poor girl aged in her disgrace
And as her eyes fell upon Time's sly face
She knew there was one challenge she could not embrace

I Will Be
by Nicolette Racz

I will be a successful woman
I wonder what my future holds
I hear people's hateful remarks chained to their jealousy
I see the long, hard road ahead, but I am determined
I want stay on the right track, but I don't know which one to choose
I pretend that I am not afraid of what the future holds
I touch the hands of those who support me and my dreams
I worry that my curious nature might get the best of me
I understand that there is lesson in every experience
I say I am brave and can conquer my dreams, but I am immature and afraid
I try to hold on to the positivity and ignore the negative aspects
that the world throws my way
I hope my hard work will pay off
I feel the people trying to pull me down,
but I am a warrior and will fight till the end
I wonder if my parents will be proud of what I accomplish
I say I am ready to open another chapter in my life, but am I really?
I understand that God has a plan for me and I will let Him lead the way
I will be a successful woman

The Struggles of Recovery
by Caitlin Russotti

Recovery can only start if you want to be helped,
While the demons within are screaming, begging to stay.
Tears sprang to my eyes as I wished them gone and let out a pleading yelp
Because I no longer wanted a life of disarray.
My still so clouded mind wanted some sunlight
To help the flower to grow inside me.
These demons, they have trapped me and made every day night;
What's it like to be free?
I screamed and screamed for them to leave
And finally the clouds moved away and out came the sun.
This! This is what I wanted to achieve,
The deflation of the demons and everyone.
Even after all the pleading for the darkness to go,
There is nothing to comfort me and I can't find the rainbow.

The Lone Wolf
by Kristina Collins

In the depth of the forest, in the midnight hour,
the white flakes fall vacantly onto the ground.
The winds blow swiftly across the land.
A full moon shimmers in the darkness of night.
In beneath the trees stands a girl.
She stands alone with only the moon's glow guiding her.
Her eyes glisten in the light of the moon.
She screams and shouts, she howls for help,
but doesn't she know the moon will not heal her spirit?
Desperately she tries to communicate with the moon,
day after day she continues to yell, grieving the loneliness she suffers with.
Even though she gets no response from the moon,
she continues to live on with her life, feeling dejected, but fighting and surviving.
Years pass and she still lies on the bed of anguish,
patiently waiting for the moon to whisper back.
She stifles her sorrow each night,
praying one day she will be able to speak to the moon.
Then, one evening, the moon was more luminous than usual.
She looked up at that moon and asked, "What am I to you?"
The moon whispered back, "You are the strength that lies beneath yourself,
you my friend are the lone wolf."

Broken Liberty
by Joshua Agbadou

What an interesting time to live in
Where what's right is deemed wrong
Where freedom of decision is now disregarded
and we are subjugated into having a forced position
Where you are "innocent until proven guilty"
yet already seen as guilty without anything proven
Where we have so many "In God We Trust" but so little trust in God
Where the saying "the land of opportunity" has drifted
because "survival of the fittest" is only suited to the richest
Where explicit music has become popularized
and there is a sudden rise in "viewer discretion is advised"
Where social media is something we prioritize
and breathe in its carbon monoxide to our own demise
It has come to a point where the truth is rejected and a lie is accepted
Will you become another one out of the 6 billion to reject this?

Poems Are Not Written For Ugly Women
by Christina Little

Ugly women do not get poems written about them, no one says they walk in beauty,
No one compares them to a summer's day, no one calls them a lily among thorns.
Not everyone can have eyes as blue as the sea,
Or hair golden like the sun, or cheeks as red as a rose.
Not everyone's laugh is like a bell,
Or nose like a button, or teeth pin straight.
Not everyone's skin is flawless like a blank canvas.
Not everyone gets love at first sight, ugly women do not.
However you cannot see kindness at first sight,
Nor humor, or brains.
You cannot see empathy at first sight,
Nor spirit, or bravery,
You cannot see personality at first sight.
If people looked more than once,
They would compare her kindness to a tender petal.
They would compare her humor to a fresh breeze, her brain to a snowflake.
They would compare her empathy to gold.
They would compare her spirit to a bird mid-flight, her bravery to a knight.
They would not be able to think of something worthy enough
to compare to her personality.
If people looked more than once, there would be more poems about ugly women.

Darkness
by Tara-Taiz Roman

Darkness surrounds me
Once everyone leaves I am alone
No one to speak to no one to listen
That's when it happens
It consumes my whole being
All I see is darkness all I feel is darkness
And I know no one can save me
Yet I always keep hope that someone will come
And once I see that sliver of light
I run to it and try to live off of it
But it vanishes and there I am
Lost in the darkness spiraling out of control until one day
It just ends

The Violet Match
by Kayla Fagerlin

As she walks into her New York City picture perfect apartment,
she realizes that her once golden red life has turned black.
Her red back shoes don't protect her anymore from the gum and dirt
that sits along the streets.
And she is alone.
Alone by herself, cut off from the billions of people in the world.
Just a red glow that walks around the big city looking for someone to love.
She tortures her eyes looking around Central Park at all the loving couples.
All the red glow wanted was to find her blue companion,
so they could make a purple footprint together.
Every night the glow sips away at a bottle of wine leaving red lip stains behind.
Until one day, a blue light shined into her life,
showing her that it was ok for her to let go sometimes,
and take off the red blush she hides behind.
No longer was she a dark maroon, but blossomed back into her golden,
bright and beautiful red.
Every morning she would put on her blue eyeliner,
and he would wear a red button-up shirt to work.
Red no longer felt isolated in world filled with people.
She was loved and useful.
And slowly but surely red and blue became one
and started parading around as purple.
Together the lavender couple lived in their bright New York City apartment.

Perfectly Imperfect
by Joelle Francisco

I am perfectly imperfect.
I trip and fall wherever I go.
I wear makeup to hide my flaws.
I am not rich nor famous.
I want what everyone else wants.
I am perfectly imperfect.
I pretend everything is okay.
I get shy around people.
I cry without hesitation.
I make millions of mistakes.
I am perfectly imperfect.
I understand that we all have insecurities.
I say, ignore other people's opinions.
I learned to love myself, and
I hope you do, too.
We are all perfectly imperfect.

Bronzed Goddess
by Mackenzie Farley

I have named you buffalo wing.
There are more flavorful than you, flavorful.
There are spicier than you, spicier.
There are juicier than you, juicier.
But you are the buffalo wing.
When everyone walks through the Super Bowl party
No one recognizes you.
No one sees your bronzy glaze, no one looks
At the pedestal of green celery
That you sit upon
The nonexistent throne.
And when I ingest you
All the rivers sound
In my body, my stomach happily
thanks me,
And a belch fills the world.
Only you and I,
Only you and I, my hot wing,
Listen to me.

Dark Beauty
by Isabella C. Nerio

Depression;
Probably the most profound, darkest thing you will encounter
We humans think we have the answers to it all
But science can't define or find the reason to why we break and fall
They say it's all mental
In reality, it's what defines us humans and our purpose of life
So beautiful, yet so dark, God put us on Earth so we can live life
The waves will get rough at times
But God guides us to restrain and to regain strength
Human life so prestige and yet so profound at times defines ...
Defines not an art but the beauty and way of life
When you think it's time to go, think twice and put away the knife
For your ambition to seek true happiness has just begun
Don't pull the plug
Don't give up
Life for you isn't done …

Code Black
by Jennyfer Mendoza

I told myself to stay away from you
But there was something in your look that made me reach for you
I told myself she would never love you
Because you seemed to be cold as snow
I took a few steps towards you
But you rushed to get away
I took a peek inside your soul
But you were quick to cover every translucent hole
There was such a gap in between us
But I tried to love you nonetheless
I tried to be oh so careful
But all I ever did was fall into the depths of your ocean blue eyes
You were ever so beautiful
A disaster I couldn't stay away from
We were so caught up in the tsunami of our love
That you made a run for it
An escape from your greatest fear; your phobia of loving too hard
And now I sit in the debris from our love
Wishing you were still here
And it is so very painful

The Light In My Life
by Purnima Prasad

His eyes are as foggy as the gray sky,
Wheat and hay blend into his hair nicely;
His naïve face can make anyone sigh;
His grin matches the grins of kids closely.
His carefree attitude and cool nature
Draws me to just admire him all day,
And his candor as a man who's mature
Makes me forget the world that is gray.
His bold, daring, and courageous actions
Cause him to be my new ideal hero,
And his epic acts are great attractions
To all people suffering from sorrow.
Though, I know he's not in God's creation;
Still, let me pull him into my nation.

A Confession
by Jasmine Sharma

When I dream tonight, I fear that it will not be of our faults, but of our joys.
I find I think of peaks only when they have aged out of their given lifetimes.
You and I are unpredictably fluid.
We flow and ebb to the tune of the week.
The salsa of the month? The waltz of the year?
The rhythm never will rest nor crescendo according to any poignant note,
But rather sway in the conductor's hand
In an obedient, vulnerable, pleading motion.
We've always been a symphony in that way.
I wish tonight, I beg, that some arousal of forgiveness
will bring you back to me in light of the discrepancy I cannot see.
The food I cannot eat.
The breath I cannot breathe.
I beg, that some miracle might be given to me.
To bring you back from your sea.
To ground your tormented vessel.
To repair your shipwreck.
I beg, that one day you'll dance again with me.
A salsa? A waltz? A sway near your sea?
When I dream tonight, I dream for you rather than for me.

Mirrors
by Emily Menjivar

The glance of a reflection
The wipe up of cover-ups
The dissatisfaction with the image left behind
The desire for a clearer and perfect you
The attempt of washing away pain
The single teardrop racing down a cold face
The last look at a body that makes one cringe
The last breath and the last tear

Rain
by Larry Chun Nok Lo

Pitter-patter, pitter-patter,
On my skin the soft droplets splatter.
One by one, from the sky they fall,
All the troubling matters, I forget them all.
The soothing drizzle, it cleanses my mind,
Healing my body, from the exhausting daily grind.
So here I stand, in the pouring rain,
It washes away, all my sorrows and pain.
Pitter-patter, pitter-patter,
The calming rain, keeps falling faster.

Black
by Jamie Ingling

I can still remember the screaming
They were arguing about money again
I could hear my mother screaming at my father,
I could hear her words clearly
"We can't afford it," he said
"I deserve better," she said
I remember them keeping the door closed,
Assuming it would muffle their voices
It didn't
I still hear the rain in my ears sometimes,
How it synchronized with my tears
There was no light outside
No sun
No hope
Black

King Moon
by Simran Kaur

Have you ever looked at the moon?
In the night sky like a bright white balloon.
The ruler of the night,
The king of shadows,
Stands high in the dark sky.
I see it every night in its new phases,
Curved with craters it has its own graces.
Its pits and scars can't affect its beauty,
And even the thickest clouds can hide its presence,
Which is visible to all in the silent night.
The moonlight lightens our path,
As full moon stands whiter than the sun
in the black starry night.
In the dark land of dreams,
Under the black sky,
The moon is our only friend,
Watching us from the heights of success.

The Confession of the First Man
by Joshua Wieder

I can hear them now ...
The growls of cryptic demons,
Sent from the deserted crevice
Where an ancient race of men once retired their hate and fear.
Grown from here are beasts of fire
Who this day cometh to end the Earth
And consume all that is.
It was me ...
Who stole the fruit off of the tree.
Not the spawn of my rib, as I claimed.
You should not have called me Adam,
You should not have sparked my spirit.
I should have remained forever devoid of light
And bereft of conscience.
Dear Lord,
You never should have made me.
Dear Lord,
You never should have made me.

Winter's Wind
by Ife Campbell

Shall I compare him to a winter's wind,
I attempt to move this way and he blasts me in the opposite direction,
I wish for warmth but his icy skin is all I feel,
I tried to lock myself away,
And wait for spring's pollen and soft breeze,
yet I could not stand avoiding my snowman.
His eyes a clear basic blue,
Like the Arctic Sea.
His voice harsh and biting,
Yet I would never leave him for a summer's day,
I stay.
In hopes that he may,
Freeze time so that forever could happen.

Smile
by Dominique Wiktorowski

Get out of bed. Smile.
You made it to another day. You woke up.
You decided to put the razor down last night. Smile.
You have to go to school soon. Go get ready. Smile.
You get to see those friends of yours another day.
But are they really your friends?
How many days can you put that smile on
Then go home and cry yourself to sleep?
How long until they notice? Smile. You can't let them know.
Laugh it off. Only a few more hours left.
But no one ever picks you so you think you're not good enough. Smile.
You are brave. You are tough. Smile.
Go home. Look in the mirror. You are beautiful, don't you see?
Smile. You are worth the life you are planning to take away soon.
Smile until you see all your self-made flaws.
Cry now. Cry until your whole world is nothing but a cold, wet blur.
Cry until you smile.
Smile because you can do it. Smile because you matter.
You can't leave today. You mean the world to me.
Put the razor down. Smile.
Make it through another day so you can smile again tomorrow.

Modern Encyclopedia
by Alexandra Volgyesi

I've been visiting the library for weeks,
Borrowing prepackaged personalities,
Fairly used, in good condition,
[They haven't been checked out recently,]
[Thankfully,]
There's been much competition for originality,
I can't help it that I'm possessive,
I need to be,
I don't get much recognition
For dressing a little messy
In my matching pair of empty identities.
I feed my eyes with visions
I need to see,
Dip fingertips into unconvention
Religiously,
Attend the Church of Unorthodox,
There is no other kind;
It's difficult to find meaning
In a world so meaninglessly divine.

They Are People
by Stefanie Osorio

They are people who travel to this country
Clutching their dreams to their hearts
They are people who travel to this country
Grasping onto hope as it slowly falls apart
Where people see illegals
I see people who took a chance
Where people see delinquents
I see the sweat of hard-workers
They are people who travel to this country
Just to be exposed by the inhumanity of others
They are people who travel to this country
Just to be judged because of their cultures
Where people see weaklings
I see people with great bravery
Where people see misfits
I see brothers and sisters
They are people who travel to this country
That are told to leave this … the land of the free
They are people who travel to this country
That are human beings just like you and me

Broken Kindness
by Esther Butler

Gesturing a wave
Warms the little girl's heart
She smiles
Offers to share her only sand shovel
With her brother
He smiles
Inspired, he turns to his mother
Appreciating the cool drink
She stares blankly, returns to her book
Breaking the chain of kindness
He scorns, kicks sand
Destroying his sister's castle
A frown forms
Hot tears roll
Down her soft cheeks
A passerby's wave
Ignored by
Sister
Brother
And Mother

Broken Boy
by Maegan Duran

I didn't know him, but it felt like I did.
His eyes, shielded by dark lashes, held secrets- secrets that broke him,
yet made him whole.
With him traveled stories- stories of how he became so damaged, stories about why
he didn't love, stories about why he had to be alone.
I'd shut my ears and tune them out because when I looked at him, I saw the truth.
Every scar on his wrist tallied the times he had cried that week.
Every time he sat alone symbolized what he was used to at home.
Every unanswered test was for every unanswered prayer.
He spoke to me once. He caught me staring at him. When his tall body walked
toward me, I felt my heart stop. He stood in front of me and watched me with his
dark fragmented eyes. "Thank you." He spoke softly.
"For what?" I questioned.
"For seeing me." And with that, he walked out of my life forever.
He was a broken boy with a tainted soul. But, to me, he was too good for this world,
because someone that painfully beautiful only has a place among the angels

I Wish I Did Something
by Marina Ghobrial

I know a friend
Who used to be bullied here.
She cried and lesser courage appeared
It troubles me to see her this way
I wish I did something-
She stopped coming to school
and changed her appearance.
She felt not good enough
and looked crushed daily.
I wish I did something-
One day she ran away
never heard of again.
It broke my heart
and I still miss her.
And always tell myself
I wish I did something

Painting
by Rebecca Zaritsky

there is a boy, in my poems
i created him with words
rather than a paintbrush.
when i am closing my eyes,
i see his looking back at me,
green eyes;electric green.
i know he has green eyes.
i have never met a boy
with green eyes.
nor have i met a boy
whose touch was so gentle,
whose smile was simultaneously
stunning and soft.
I have never met a boy
who I loved quite so much
as the boy in my poetry.

Four Seasons
by Kaitlyn Bosch

An immense, golden orb sits.
It stares, conflagrant.
Wilting flesh and stems abound.
The slow breeze traverses down;
The orb shrinks, and falls.
A biting chill licks my lips.
Scarves, shovels, and souvenirs
Evade solitude.
Waiting for flowers to bloom.
I grow; it grows; but we don't.
The shade stays quiet;
Watching the blooming daylight.

In the Eyes of the Light
by Mariamu Kesselly

There's this creature that walks among us
It can pretend and act just like us
Yes it has legs and arms
And we all feel it will cause us harm
Its skin as black as a blank night sky
Its tongue of language is the tongue of lies
We attempt to restrain it
Or even oppress it
And after this we hope for extinction
So we can lead the world in our direction
They repopulate furiously in front of our eyes
But while they increase many of us die
They're ignorant, ill-mannered and never neat
Their weakness is sugar water and boneless meat
They refuse to wear clothes the right way
We all lay quiet in its presence for days
Their eyes and their lives are stained with sin
I think I speak for those with dirt less skin

Four New Yorkers' Views On Prada
by Jacqueline Butler

I. Passing "them" on the bus every morning,
They see a flash of angry birds.
Or maybe birds instructed to look angry.
Supercilious peacocks!
Wearing the variegated plumage of Prada fashion.
II. He changes the poster every six weeks.
His mouth falls open!
The Prada handbag dangling from the bejeweled wrist
Costs twice his monthly wage;
Symbolic of the elusive American Dream.
III. His wife longs for the gold and silver threads
Woven into a stunning masterpiece.
But her heart reaches out to the lonely figure.
And she is grateful for her lot,
Which does not include Prada dresses.
IV. I can buy her pumps but can I have her figure?
I will! I will!
This image-conscious girl walks up E. 70th to hail a cab
Thinks better of it
And runs to prep school in Prada flats

Caramel Brown
by Malaya Grant

Caramel brown is the complexion that makes me unique,
That can tell people of the world series that they may have never heard
Caramel brown is the foundation that covers my exterior, a color
That was said to be inferior to the white race, colored blood
Running through my veins, deemed by ancestors to be slaves,
From the beautiful African women,to the graceful Native Americans
Who sung their rituals of nature and love, because they knew that the God
From above would take them from their Hell of Earth,
From the human stain that marked hopelessness on their foreheads
And "Runaways" on their arms, my skin tone is a variation of dark and light
But it doesn't tell me what complexion is wrong or right
But it shows how far blood has gone and much farther it will go
Because the reflections that we see in the mirror, help to unfold the blankets
Covering our identity, that was overlooked by the sensitivity that we had]
When we were told, that no shade of brown was good enough
That we shouldn't trust what our God created in us, but caramel brown
Don't ever look down, because your skin is light, enough to show the miracles
That God has done, but dark enough to hold up the sun

If I Won the Lottery
by Shadwine Pierre

If I won the lottery
I would buy mama the house she dreamed
about when she was 12
I would buy her the car that I dreamed about
when I was 12
If I won I would go out and buy a house
for homeless people to live in
If I won I would buy my dad his own house
on the islands of Haiti
If I won I would buy homes that couldn't
be brought down by a 7.0 magnitude
earthquake
If I won I would bring America to my aunt and uncles
that are forced to stay on the Islands of Misery

Love At First Sight
by Jenna Monid

As her radiant eyes gaze around the room
Let them meet with yours and let the games resume
Carefully after meeting with yours, her eyes will look away
Significantly, this is a sign that she wants yours to stay
Her eyes will do the talking, by screaming out their history
This will be a giveaway that she is nothing but a mystery
Your chore is to be the detective, and go crack the case
In no time at all, you'll know there is no time to waste
Eyelashes intertwined with mascara will take your breath away
And when she's biting her lip, you'll know she has something to say
Time to approach her, and you'll take it slow
She'll prove to you momentarily where she wants this to go
At first chance you smile an infamous grin
And in return, you get only a lift of her chin
She walks away and is now taken from your view
Unlike Cinderella, she does not leave behind a shoe
The girl with the eyes telling stories to you
Was gone in the time that that autumn wind blew
You walk on, alone, thinking it couldn't have been right
After all, there is no such thing as love at first sight.

An Immigrant Living In America
by Avosuahi Albert

Memories can be beautiful, memories can be ugly
Coming from the motherland where poverty
war and lack of self run rampant as a failure
to human society. I hear of a place called America, which I call
the promised land, where equality, opportunity and freedom exist.
Through the motherland I hear whispers in the air that weaken my goals and
freedom, freedom to speak, say how I feel, but end up getting closed up in the box.
Only the rich matter and the poor are like skunks
with no future security is not granted.
In the mother-land the government promises the people better lives
but watches the nation bleed.
As the world collapses under the weight of what money can't sometimes solve.
Oh why has greed, war, violence taken over my land
I escape to America with my family to seek a better life
there is crisis everywhere one goes but use the opportunity you are given
and make good use of it.

The World Wants Grey
by Megan Schaffner

The world wants grey. Be bleak, the sky on a damp, endless afternoon
bogged down with mist, the silence that blends you into oblivion,
the stained, dull pavement so worn from being trampled on that it just sits.
Because those who stand out get shut down.
Those with imaginations and wings of color and light,
who soar over plains and valleys, are strange.
Crazy, they are, who live as if their souls are on fire
and to extinguish the flames is to suffocate them as well.
But label me Heathcliff.
Let the monomania consume every ounce of my being,
clench every inch of my lungs
until there is no space left for life, no room left for breathing.
The pain of losing my Catherine is preferable
to the agony of never having loved her at all.
Every beat of my heart parallels another's last,
so why waste moments half-felt and hues half-seen?
Bring not your boat to the shoreline, but allow the waves to consume you.
Let three words be your oxygen; let your heart, frozen or burning, fester to the point
of explosion so that your footsteps fossilize behind you.
Nurture your passion so that the world is exhausted when your time comes.
Otherwise, you will have never experienced life at all.

On Growing Up
by Elizabeth Bottoni

Her youth has passed in song and light and fire
Her eyes pass o'er her new and strengthened form
In way of morals she shall never tire
Finding her own path she is often torn
A girl, once slight and small and smart and proud
Incredibly had only slightly changed
She challenged limits, found her way in crowds
Her body and her mind just slightly aged
And though success someday seems like a lie
She need only wait for her time and try

The Man I Used To Know ...
by Alexandra Duran

He was different before it happened
He used to smile a sweet smile
His eyes were soft and light and beautiful
He loved traveling and adventures
He was always happy and showed kindness to everyone
He had so many friends and everyone loved him
He was the greatest man I ever met
After it happened he was different
Now he rarely smiles, and when he does it's not like it was
His eyes are surrounded by dark circles, they are always weary
and are filled with sadness and exhaustion
He is always tired, exhausted, in pain, and sad
He pushes his friends away because he doesn't want them to see him like this
He is the strongest man I ever met
I've tried to bring him back with love, but it's not enough.
He can't live like this anymore, and I know that, I just don't want to accept it.
He doesn't want to feel tired anymore.
He doesn't want to feel pain every second of the day anymore.
He doesn't want to fight for his life anymore.
He just wants to be free. I will miss him forever.
I know he loves me even though he must go. I'm finally ready to let him go.
He is the brave man I used to know

Daniel Johnson

The Robin's Egg
by Daniel Johnson

It rests in the valley of my palm,
plucked from the dirt like a blue dandelion–
the robin's egg blessed with the color of the sky.
Ignorant of its fragility, its thinness,
I wrap it in a green towel. Perfect blue
nestled in manufactured linen– a makeshift nest.
Teal and aquamarine are not compatible.
Madly I reach for it,
longing for the weight of beauty, of life.
It cracks under the pressure of my fascination.
Mucus apprehends my fingers.
Holding a planet tortured by earthquakes
which I have caused,
blue shards overwhelm my teary vision
as the cracks quickly become broken glass edges.
Finches and robins taunt me
with chirped shrieks of mocking:
reminders of what could have been
if I had not broken
the robin's egg.

2nd Place

Tara Holz

Through a Mother's Eyes
by Tara Holz

Look at that little girl in the backseat,
Not more than three feet tall,
Plastic tiara perched on a head of vivacious blonde curls,
Clutching a pack of sticky fruit snacks,
Wide eyes almost touching a nose-smudged window.
Only a few seconds pass until my next glance,
But she's already grown out of her car seat,
slumped against the leather,
Thick eyeliner and black from head to boot,
Eyes the same shade as mine glued to her pristine phone,
Earbuds plugged in, stoutly tuned out,
Not listening, not listening, not listening.
My little girl shoves me into the passenger seat, grabs the wheel,
She speeds up– no, slow down!– defiant eyes locked forward.
Cluttered backseat– tap shoes, tennis racket, waitress apron,
A disregarded pile of her who-I-used-to-be's.
I envision her metamorphosis once she's far from here:
Shiny Louboutins, starched blouse, wild locks pinned back too tightly.
She tenses at my inquisitive gaze and notches up the radio.
So I silently sit back, massaging my arthritic fingers,
And pray she lets her hair down once in a while.

1st Place

Devany Shikiar

Devany submitted her poem while in the tenth grade.
Her love of reading and writing is apparent,
as is the importance she places on family.
Her poem, "Strawberry Birthmark"
is not only very well written,
but is a poignant portrayal
of how all parents struggle to shelter their children
from the sometimes cruel harshness of the real world.
We are pleased to present the work of Devany Shikiar,
our 2016 Editor's Choice Award Winner.

Editor's Choice Award

Strawberry Birthmark
by Devany Shikiar

Strawberry birthmark.
A red stain of paint
that could neither be erased with soap nor the saltwater of tears.
It's from your father and me kissing you too much,
my mother would say.
Too many kisses, I'd tell laughing faces.
Too much love, I'd tell the mocking voices.
Strawberry birthmark,
an invader of pale innocent skin and a magnet for insults.
They're just jealous we love you so much, my father would say,
and they'd kiss me until the tears turned into laughter.
Even with rough washcloths and scalding water,
my strawberry birthmark stayed.
It wasn't until the fighting began and the kisses stopped
that it began to fade.
Strawberry birthmark.
It was an unfit red splotch that could be erased.
Erased with too little love and too few kisses.
A strawberry birthmark finally erased,
left a greater absence in its place.

Index
of
Authors

Index of Authors

Index of Authors

I

Ibarasa, Hezekiah 35
Ibraimi, Marisa 20
Iino, Paige 50
Inghrim, Lindsay 41
Ingling, Jamie 203
Ionta, Anthony 153

J

Jacobs, Molly 18
Jadon, Ishita 68
Jaworski, Nicholas 87
Jenkins, Tiara 80
Jessin, Liam 4
Johnson, Daniel 214
Johnson, Julia 24
Jorge, Alexis 34
Joseph, Daniel 12
Justin, Joshua 47

K

Kali, Patrice 96
Kang, Minji 55
Kang, Noah 55
Kasper, Frank 29
Kassam, Rose 103
Kaur, Simran 204
Keshiro, Samah 31
Kesselly, Mariamu 209
Kiessling, Quinn 53
Kim, Gaeun 133
Kim, Lauren 119
Kim, Naomi 16
Kinkead, Nolan 50
Kirk, Paige 37
Kirschner, Ella 187
Kisswani, Hana 95
Kivlehan, Mia 131
Knox, Julia 111
Koffi, Jeanne D'arc 166
Kogut, Rachel 172
Komendant, C. 192

Kopko, Connor 170
Kratz, Emily 186
Kucharski, Emma 43
Kuras, Kristiana 124
Kuriakose, Aleena 34

L

Laderas, Jason 75
Laffler, Zoe 57
Lam, Ivan 69
Lancaster, Kaya 51
Landis, Julia 98
Langhorne, Madison 24
Lanzone, Leo 34
Larsen, David 17
Lawrence, Daenna 106
Lee, Hannah 39
Lee, Maya R. 121
Lee, Yubin Martina 41
Lemley, Jack 42
Levy, Hannah 170
Linder, Jacob 56
Lipkin, Elisa 173
Little, Christina 198
Lo, Larry Chun 203
Lopes, Ana 18
Lopez, David 150
Loustan, Macie 137
Lucius, Alexa 67
Lundy, Rudolph 125

M

Magat-Carr, Seye 42
Magos, Michelle 101
Mahoney, Shaelyn 141
Malone, Benjamin 30
Mancuso, Samantha 44
Manning, Michael 90
Marcial, Zitlali 152
Marin, Sara 83
Marley, John 94
Marrapodi, S. 152
Martin, Courtney 114

Martinez, M. 185
Martini, Theresa 164
Martin, Sara 138
Martire, Kaitlyn 40
Martorano, Jade 84
Mauro, Angelina 31
McAndrews, Grace 125
McDonough, Hailey 38
McVey, Brennan 21
Melville, Hannah 194
Mendoza, Diana 69
Mendoza, Jennyfer 201
Menjivar, Emily 203
Metz, Darby 116
Miceli, Grace 147
Mills, Maryssa 75
Minde, Laurel 110
Min, Jeffrey 76
Mintel, Joey 21
Mishkin, Allie 130
Mistichelli, Dena 57
Mollica, Nicholas 157
Monid, Jenna 211
Monteleone, Colin 172
Montena, Jake 130
Moore, Grace 91
Morales, Jeremiah 151
Mori, Gabrielle 23
Morton, Jayson 35
Motyczka, Margot 127
Muller, Alana 64
Mumma, Calvin 110
Muskopf, Jamie 143

N

Nasief, Mariam 156
Navarrete, Lidia 158
Nerio, Isabella C. 201
Nezaj, Sabrina 178
Nguyen, Michelle 155
Nicholson, Kaylah 171
Niedosik, Danielle 42
No, Isabella 46

Index of Authors

Index of Authors

Accomplished
Price List

Initial Copy 32.95

Additional Copies 25.00

Please Enclose $7 Shipping/Handling Each Order

Must specify book title and name of student author

Check or Money Order Payable to:

The America Library of Poetry
P.O. Box 978
Houlton, Maine 04730

Please Allow 4-8 Weeks For Delivery

THE AMERICA
LIBRARY OF POETRY

www.libraryofpoetry.com

Email: generalinquiries@libraryofpoetry.com